CW01660449

Walk!

around

The Malverns

with

Bob Greaves

DISCOVERY WALKING GUIDES LTD

Walk! Around The Malverns
First Edition - July 2011

Copyright © 2011

Published by
Discovery Walking Guides Ltd
10 Tennyson Close, Northampton NN5 7HJ, England

Mapping supplied by **Global Mapping Limited**
(www.globalmapping.com)

This product includes mapping data licensed from **Ordnance Survey®** with the permission of the Controller of Her Majesty's Stationery Office. © Crown Copyright 2005. All rights reserved.

Licence Number 40044851

Front Cover Photographs

Down from Herefordshire Beacon (Walk 14)

Worcestershire Beacon (Walk 17)

Butcher's Row, Ledbury (Walk 21)

Eckington Bridge (Walk 5)

ISBN 9781904946762
Text and photographs © Bob Greaves

All rights reserved. No part of this publication may be reproduced, stored in a retrieval system or transmitted in any form or by any means, electronic, mechanical, photocopying, recording or otherwise, without the prior written permission of the publishers.

The author and publishers have tried to ensure that the information and maps in this publication are as accurate as possible. However, we accept no responsibility for any loss, injury or inconvenience sustained by anyone using this book.

Walk! around The Malverns

CONTENTS

THE AUTHOR

Educated at a traditional grammar school, Bob Greaves had to choose, aged thirteen, between the Science and Arts sides. As he was good at sums he chose the Science side and went on to a degree in Pure Mathematics and a career in the computer industry.

Introduced to walking and maps as a child, he has found his way independently to many parts of Britain and walked in Ireland, France, Austria, Czech Republic, Greece, Madeira (a favourite) as well as La Gomera and La Palma in the Canaries. As a walk leader, he has delighted in designing a variety of itineraries that meet the demands of different groups.

Now, with two married daughters and seven grandchildren under his belt, so to speak, he has grasped the opportunity to combine his passion with his computer experience to embark on a new career researching and writing walking books.

ACKNOWLEDGEMENTS

Firstly, I want to thank the generous individuals who gave my **Walk! the Brecon Beacons** such positive reviews on Amazon. Their various comments reflected all that I had tried to achieve in writing that book and encouraged me no end. Also I'd given a copy to proof-reader Sally-Mae's ninety-seven year old father and discovered that he'd read it from cover to cover, following the routes of all 40 walks in his imagination - what a revelation!

The research and writing was done in two parts, the first 18 walks in 2006/7 when Sally-Mae was a great support but the project was put on hold when I moved away from the area. On my return in 2010, besides researching an additional 12 walks, I rewalked the original 18 and Moth accompanied me on most of them to highlight what had changed and laugh at some of the observations I had made.

Finally, thank you again, Ros and David, for your ongoing support.

INTRODUCTION

When I first met the publishers, David and Ros Brawn of Discovery Walking Guides, this is the book that I wanted to produce but at that time they were keen to have a guide to the Brecon Beacons and so **Walk! the Brecon Beacons** was born. Following its success, they agreed to publish the book you're now reading, **Walk! Around the Malverns** which is simply a record of all my favourite walks carefully described and annotated following their now familiar strict guidelines. For many years I have lived in the area, first in the lee of **Bredon Hill** and now in **Malvern Wells** where I walk out of my back door up onto the ridge of the hills almost every day.

Upton Upon Severn

There are thirty great walks here, ranging from a gentle stroll along the **River Severn** from **Upton upon Severn** to a strenuous hike along the complete length of the **Malvern Hills** including all its summits.

The Malvern Hills

My aim througout is to inspire confidence. Perhaps you've only ventured out on walks with a group, concerned that you might get lost, armed with this book and a GPS you need have no such fears.

I've tackled each one of these walks in the last year and the routes shown on the maps are the precise routes I took, recorded on a GPS - for those without a GPS, each walk includes detailed route descriptions and the grid coordinates of every waypoint.

THE AREA COVERED

Overbury

Starting in the east, there are five walks over **Bredon Hill**, a neglected walking area in my opinion, enhanced by its encircling string of delightful villages, many with great country pubs. A gentle walk around **Pershore** follows and then a longer walk which visits **Tewkesbury.** South of **Tewkesbury**, another stroll

Tewkesbury Abbey

visits three memorable churches and three pubs linked together by a river, then a visit to **Upton on Severn** is followed by two interesting walks into and out of **Worcester**.

The Severn at Worcester

Two leisurely walks over the **Severn Plain** lead us onto The Malverns proper where Walks 14 to 24 criss-cross the hills in a myriad of different ways, hopefully finding some delights that even seasoned locals haven't discovered.

The Worcestershire Beacon

Next we explore **Old Storridge Common** to the north, go over **Oyster Hill** to **Ledbury** and follow **The Daffodil Way** around **Dymock**.

The River Wye

At our western extremity two walks take us as far as the **River Wye** and our concluding adventure is up ever-popular **May Hill**.

WHERE TO STAY

Great Malvern is the obvious place to stay and for a wide choice of accommodation visit **www.great-malvern.co.uk** or the excellent Tourist Information Centre (01684 802289) at the top of the town. For the walks over **Bredon Hill**, **Tewkesbury** or one of the hill's encircling villages is a good choice. For what it's worth, I have personal experience of several places and these are detailed in Appendix B at the back of the book.

HISTORY

The **Herefordshire Beacon** aka **British Camp** is an impressive iron age hill-fort which had a medieval motte and bailey castle in the 11th and 12th centuries

Herefordshire Beacon

Remnants of Shire Ditch

Earthworks along the ridge of **The Malvern Hills** were dug in 1287 and are called the **Shire Ditch** or **Red Earl's Dyke**. They were built by Gilbert de Clare, the 3rd Earl of Gloucester to protect hunting rights from his neighbour Thomas de Cantiloupe, the Bishop of Hereford and were cunningly designed so that deer could jump over it onto his land but not back again.

In 1884, the Malvern Hills Conservators were formed to conserve the area as common land for both locals and visitors. Most importantly, they limited the scale of quarrying which threatened to alter the hills'famous outline. Now they have the difficult task of balancing the ecological needs of the area with an ever growing army of visitors

Great Malvern itself dates from 1085 when a Benedictine Priory was built. But it's emergence as a famous spa town was due to the recognition of the purity of water collected from the many springs that surround the hills and the discovery of the 'water cure' by Doctors Wilson and Gully.

Holywell Spring

This consisted of plenty of fresh Malvern Water, lots of exercise and a strict diet free of alcohol and rich foods, probably the reason for its success. But it also involved having cold showers and being entwined in wet sheets - less likely to be efficacious. The establishment of renowned schools for both boys in 1865 and girls in 1893 brought further expansion and during the second world war the government centre for radar research (now privately owned **Qinetiq**) came to the town and attracted many intelligent and interesting characters to the area.

Old Pershore Bridge

The Severn Plain is particularly remembered for the Battles of Worcester and Tewkesbury towards the end of the civil war. During the king's flight from Oxford back to Worcester, the bridge over the **River Avon** at **Pershore** was destroyed to hold up the Roundheads and its hurried repair can be clearly seen to this day.

GEOLOGY

.. looking west ..

The Malvern Hills are formed of rocks from the Pre-Cambrian era, some maybe 1,000 million years old. Their hardness explains why the hills stick up so prominently from the surrounding landscape. About 300 million years ago faults which later became the ways across the hills of **The Wyche** and **The Gullet** were formed. When standing on the ridge of the hills the geology of the land to east and west is clearly diametrically different. To the west the undulating landscape is of Silurian rocks formed 400 million years ago but to the east the flat **Severn Plain** is formed of sands and clays from the Permo-Triassic period *only* 250 million years ago.

.. looking east ..

THE ROUTES

The order of the walks is roughly from east to west. Each of the routes consist of a summary, some key information described in the Symbols Rating Guide (see an explanation of the guide on page 14) how to get to the start and a detailed description which includes timings at each waypoint. Every walk has its own OS mapping with the route and its key waypoints clearly overlaid.

The timings are those that I actually did, minus the time taken for any stops. Obviously you're likely to walk faster or slower than me, so I suggest you walk a couple of the easier, shorter walks first and see how your times compare with mine so that you can factor that in.

ACCESS BY CAR

Directions are always from the most convenient motorway junction, there's never one far away as the M5 and M50 cut right through the area covered. Clearly this is good for those travelling from outside the area, not so good for those staying in the area but at least it gives a readily identifiable place to start directions from. A grid reference and postcode are also given for entering into satellite navigation systems; but be aware that postcodes are designed for delivering post so if there are no residences near the start of a walk entering a postcode will only get you to the nearest residence.

ACCESS BY PUBLIC TRANSPORT

Wherever possible I've endeavoured to find a way of getting to the walks by public transport. This is not always to the walks'start but as most walks are circular this is no big deal. However, in these changing times, there is no guarantee that bus routes described will still be running by the time you're reading this. I find that www.travelinemidlands.co.uk is a really practical website for bus or rail timetables. For those without cars I've brought together the 'Access by Public Transport' details of all walks in Appendix A.

GPS ANOMALIES

Contrary to myth, perhaps spread by the anti-GPS brigade, I found no deterioration of GPS performance in adverse weather conditions. Where it did become an issue was where dense trees completely covered the way, particularly when this was combined with being on the side of a hill.

Routes affected were:-

Walk 15 Between Great Malvern and Colwall Stations	Wp.10 to Wp.13
Walk 16 North Hill from Link Common	Wp.14 to Wp.19
Walk 17 Worcestershire Beacon	Wp.12 to Wp.15
Walk 18 Holywell and 'The Kettle Sings'	Wp.1 to Wp.6 and Wp.12 back to Wp.1
Walk 28 Old Storridge Common	Wp.2 to Wp.5, Wp.18 to Wp.20 and Wp.24 back to Wp.1

WALK LOCATORMAPS

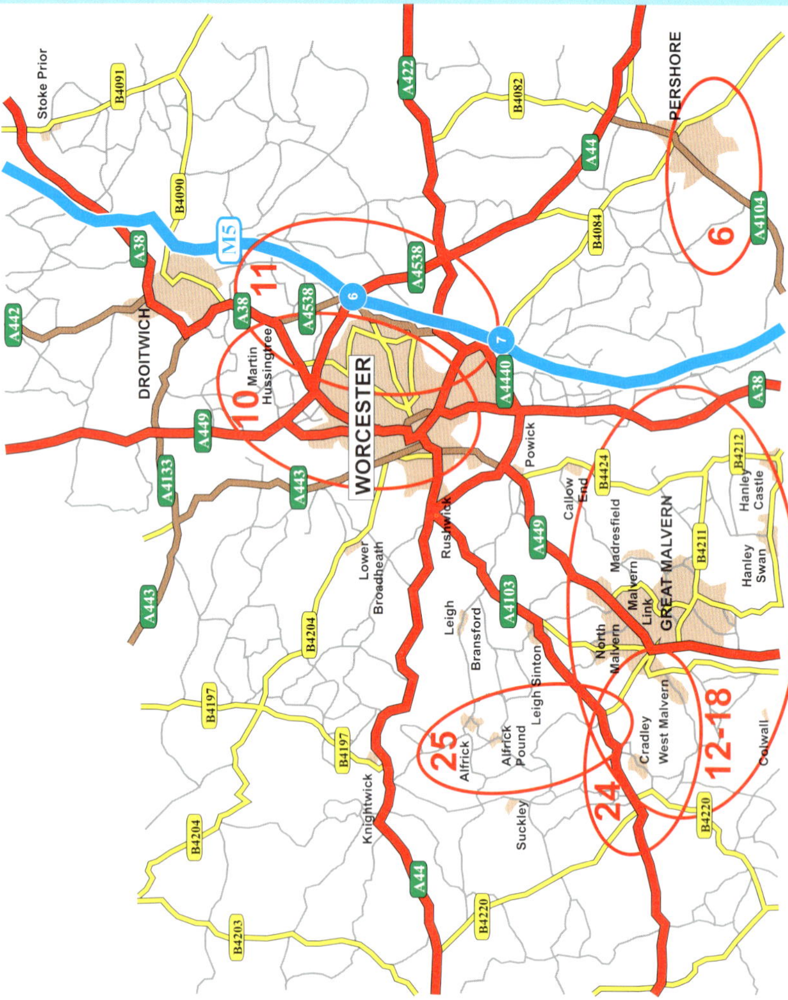

Approximate area covered in
Walk! Around the Malverns

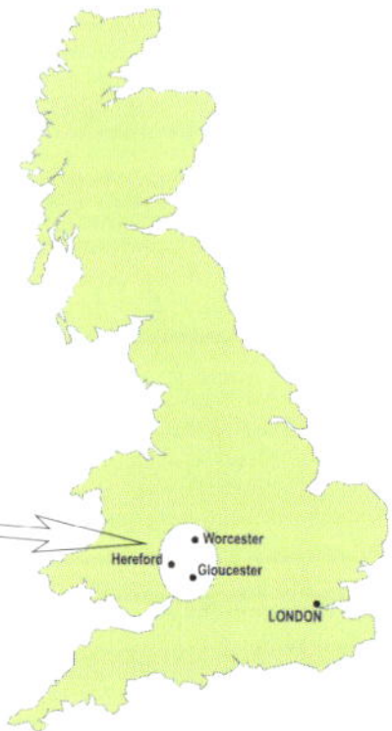

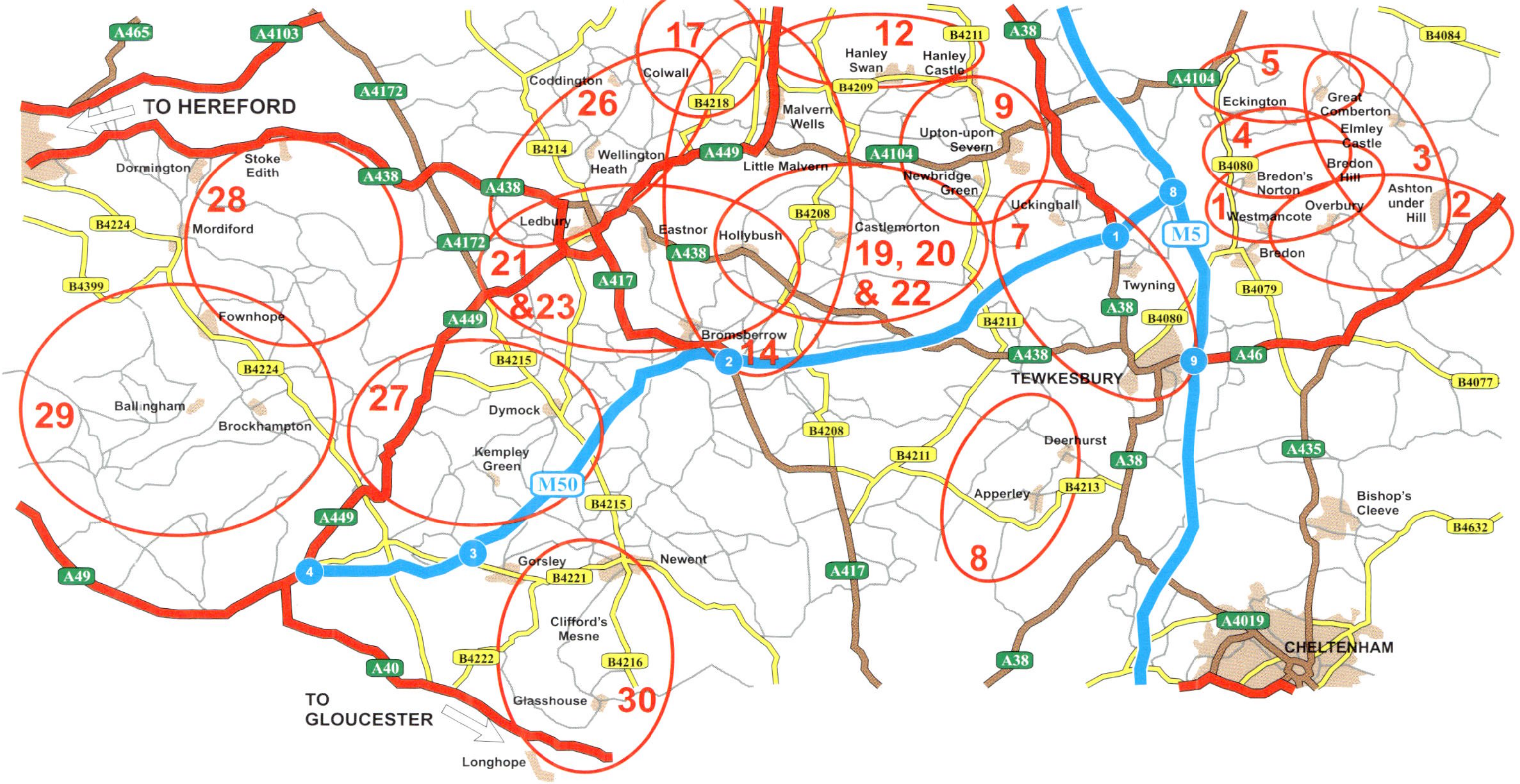

TO HEREFORD
TO GLOUCESTER
Dormington
Stoke Edith
Mordiford
Fownhope
Ballingham
Brockhampton
Coddington
Colwall
Wellington Heath
Ledbury
Malvern Wells
Little Malvern
Eastnor
Hollybush
Bromsberrow
Hanley Swan
Hanley Castle
Upton-upon Severn
Newbridge Green
Castlemorton
Uckinghall
Twyning
Tewkesbury
Deerhurst
Apperley
Dymock
Kempley Green
Gorsley
Newent
Clifford's Mesne
Glasshouse
Longhope
Eckington
Great Comberton
Elmley Castle
Bredon Hill
Bredon's Norton
Westmancote
Overbury
Ashton under Hill
Bredon
Bishop's Cleeve
CHELTENHAM
M5
M50
A465
A4103
A4172
A438
A449
A417
A4104
A38
A46
A435
A4019
A49
A40
B4224
B4399
B4214
B4218
B4209
B4211
B4208
B4215
B4221
B4222
B4216
B4213
B4080
B4079
B4077
B4084
B4632
1
2
3
4
5
7
8
9
12
14
17
19, 20 & 22
21 & 23
26
27
28
29
30

SYMBOLS RATING GUIDE

3 our rating for effort/exertion:- **1** very easy **2** easy **3** average **4** energetic **5** strenuous

2½ H approximate **time** to complete a walk (compare your times against ours early in a walk) - does not include stopping time

5 miles/8km approximate walking **distance** in miles/kilometres

250m 850m approximate **ascents/descents** in metres (N=negligible)

circular route

linear route

figure of eight route

risk of **vertigo**

3 **refreshments** (may be at start or end of a route only)

- Walk descriptions include:
- timing in minutes, shown as (40M)
- compass directions, shown as (NW)
- heights in metres, shown as (1355m)
- GPS waypoints, shown as (Wp.3)

Notes on the text

Place names are shown in **bold text**, except where we refer to a written sign, when they are enclosed in single quotation marks. Local or unusual words are shown in *italics*, and are explained in the accompanying text.

ORDNANCE SURVEY MAPPING

All the map sections which accompany the detailed walk descriptions in Walk! Around The Malverns are reproduced under Ordnance Survey licence from the digital versions of the latest Explorer 1:25,000 scale maps. Walking Route and GPS Waypoints are then drawn onto the map section to produce the map illustrating the detailed walk description.

Walk! Around The Malverns map sections are sufficient for following the detailed walk descriptions, but for planning your adventures in this region we strongly recommend that you purchase the latest OS Explorer maps.

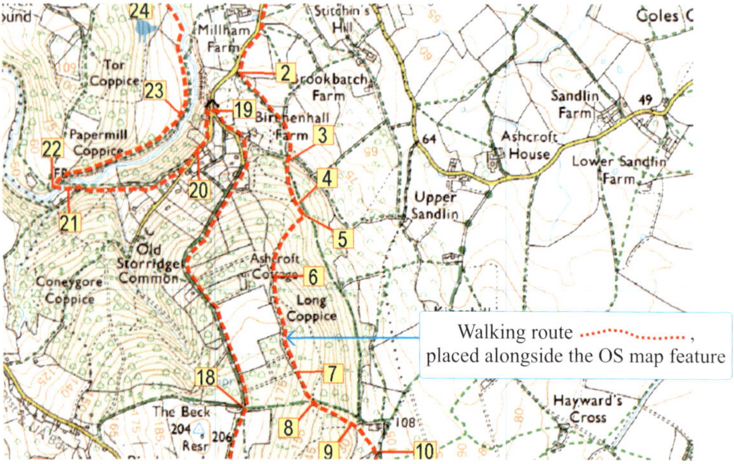

The GPS Waypoint lists provided in this book are as recorded by Bob Greaves while researching the detailed walk descriptions. Waypoint symbols are numbered so that they can be directly identified with the walk description and waypoint list. All GPS Waypoints are subject to the accuracy of GPS units in the particular location of each waypoint.

In the dramatic landscapes of the Malvern Hills, GPS reception is surprisingly good for the majority of Bob's walking routes.

Satellite Reception
Accurate location fixes for your GPS unit depend upon you receiving signals from four or more satellites. Providing you have good batteries, and that you wait until your GPS has full 'satellite acquisition' before starting out, your GPS will perform well in the Malvern Hills. Where Bob has encountered poor satellite reception it is mentioned in the walk description and on page 11.

Manually Inputting Waypoints
GPS Waypoints are quoted for the OSGB (Ordnance Survey Great Britain) datum and BNG (British National Grid) coordinates, making them identical with the OS grid coordinates of the position they refer to.
To manually input the Waypoints into your GPS we suggest that you:

- switch on your GPS and select 'simulator/standby/'use with gps off'' mode
- check that your GPS is set to the OSGB datum and BNG 'location/position format'
- input the GPS Waypoints into a 'gps route' with the same number as the walking route; then when you call up the 'route' in the Malvern Hills there will be no confusion as to which walking route it refers
- repeat the inputting of waypoints into 'gps routes' until you have covered all the routes you plan to walk, or until you have used up the memory capacity of your GPS
- turn off your GPS. When you turn your GPS back on it should return to its normal navigation mode.

Note that GPS Waypoints complement the routes in Walk! The Malverns, and are not intended as an alternative to the detailed walking route descriptions.

Personal Navigator Files (PNFs) CD
Edited versions of Bob's original GPS research tracks and waypoints are available as downloadable files on our PNFs CD (version 6.01), which includes the edited GPS records for all the Walk!/Walks guide books published by DWG along with GPS Utility Special edition software. See DWG websites for more information:

www.walking.demon.co.uk & www.dwgwalking.co.uk

GPS The Easy Way (£4.99)
If you are confused by talk of GPS, but are interested in how this modern navigational aid could enhance your walking enjoyment, then simply seek out a copy of GPS The Easy Way, the UK's best selling GPS manual.

WALKING EQUIPMENT

Most importantly, walk with what you feel comfortable in. What follows are some of my personal choices.

- **Feet** must be comfortable - I usually wear boots which are lightweight but still waterproof with two pairs of socks but when it's warm enough I love to walk in sandals which have improved no end in the last few years.

- **Rucksack** - as small and lightweight as possible, the only other condition being that it must be waterproof, most easily accomplished by the use of a waterproof liner.

- **Sunstroke** - even when it's cloudy I wear a hat during the summer, though I have to admit that it's more crucial if you have a bald spot on top!

- **Dehydration** - not taking enough water is a temptation because it is so heavy. I drink plenty before setting out and then little and often, remember that feeling thirsty is your body telling you that you are beginning to dehydrate. Making the water easily available helps; the method by which a tube hangs permanently in front of your face from a pouch in your rucksack may look naff but works well.

- **Energy** - in addition to my packed lunch I take an oatmeal bar, chocolate and dried fruit. As well as supplying a quick energy boost they are welcomed by companions.

- Rain - I have waterproof, lightweight, breatheable tops and bottoms that are quick to put on when the rain starts, the important lesson is to put them on at the first hint of precipitation even if it looks as though it will only last five minutes.

- **Keeping warm** - If it's a warm day I'll just wear a T-shirt, if cooler a shirt and fleece. Either way, I pack a pullover, gloves and a woolly hat that I can pull down over my ears.

- **GPS** with spare batteries.

- **Emergencies** - Take a loud whistle. The internationally recognized distress signal is six long blasts in quick succession at one minute intervals. Don't assume you will be able to get a signal on your mobile - but still be sure to take it!

- **Other things** - Plasters, mozzie cream, suncream, tissues

- **Final thought** : If you suddenly need something while in the area I can thoroughly recommend Harper's Bazaar on the Worcester Road in Malvern Link which is like an Aladdin's Cave. The helpful staff will happily sell you a single tent peg - it's that sort of place!

1 BREDON HILL FROM WESTMANCOTE

Bredon Hill falls very much in the shadow of the **Malvern Hills** as a walking destination yet has much to commend it, not least the encircling string of attractive villages, many with satisfying pubs. This walk is a personal favourite, starting gently across farmland, then up through **Westmancote** climbing ever steeper to straddle the ridge along to the tower. Then it's down to the picture book village of **Overbury**, along past the lake in the grounds of **Kemerton Court** to **The Crown** in **Kemerton** before returning along wood and field paths to our start.

Access by car:
From junction 9 of the M5 head towards **Evesham** on the A46 and at traffic lights, turn left onto the B4079 to **Bredon**. In the village turn left and then right onto the A4080 to **Pershore**. Shortly after leaving the village **Bredon Hill** is visible ahead on the right; park in a large lay-by on the left. OS Grid reference : SO 92798 37496 Nearest postcode : GL20 7HE.

Access by bus:
Bus N°540 runs from **Tewkesbury** to **Evesham**; alight at **Lower Westmancote** and follow the instructions from Wp.26 to Wp.3 and start the circuit from there. Bus users have the option of shortening the walk by bussing back from either **Overbury** (Wp.20 160M) or **Kemerton** (Wp.24 192M).

From the lay-by (Wp.1 0M) we start by heading back towards **Bredon** (SSW) on the right hand grass verge diametrically away from our objective of **Bredon Hill** with the tall spire of **Bredon** church appearing above tree tops. Shortly after passing a bungalow, we cross the road and follow a public footpath signpost up a bank and through a kissing gate (Wp.2 3M). Our way is on the flat across a field (ENE) with a row of trees on our left - now we're going more in the right direction! Reaching a metal gate, we cross a lane (Wp.3 11M) and follow a footpath signposted 'Westmancote' which runs between the large gardens of houses either side. Through the hedge to the right we can see an impressive 'model' railway and particularly admire the station of 'Frog Furlong Spa' with its old metal advertisements. Passing into a field, we continue in the same direction towards the buildings of **Westmancote**, veering right at the far side of the field towards a road (Wp.4 19M). Meeting it, we turn left by a converted chapel and begin to climb gently (NE) peering into the gardens of some desirable properties.

After passing **Chapel Lane** and then **Farm Lane** we climb steadily steeper until, ignoring signposted footpaths both straight on and to the left, we swing right (Wp.5 34M E) to enjoy great views over the hedge. Where the lane swings back left (NNE) it becomes an unmade track and we continue climbing steadily until we arrive at a fork (Wp.6 41M) and take the left, blue waymarked option (N). For a short time the way becomes steeper but flattens out after swinging left (W) and then immediately right (N).

But before long we begin to climb again, gently at first then steadily up passing between gateposts. Ignoring a track that goes down to the left opposite a 'No Right of Way' sign forbidding our entry to a wood, we complete another short steep section before passing through a further pair of gateposts into a large expanse of grassland (Wp.7 58M). The reward for this significant climb is a panoramic view; **Westmancote** is below us, **Bredon** beyond and the white roofs of the modern industrial area of **Northway** stand out in front of **Tewkesbury Abbey**. To the right, the **River Avon** passes under the motorway before meandering its way around the hill.

Our route onward goes right (NE) to follow a green swathe beside a tumbledown dry stone wall. Passing through a wooden gate we continue by the wall, now with a mysterious looking wood on the other side of it.

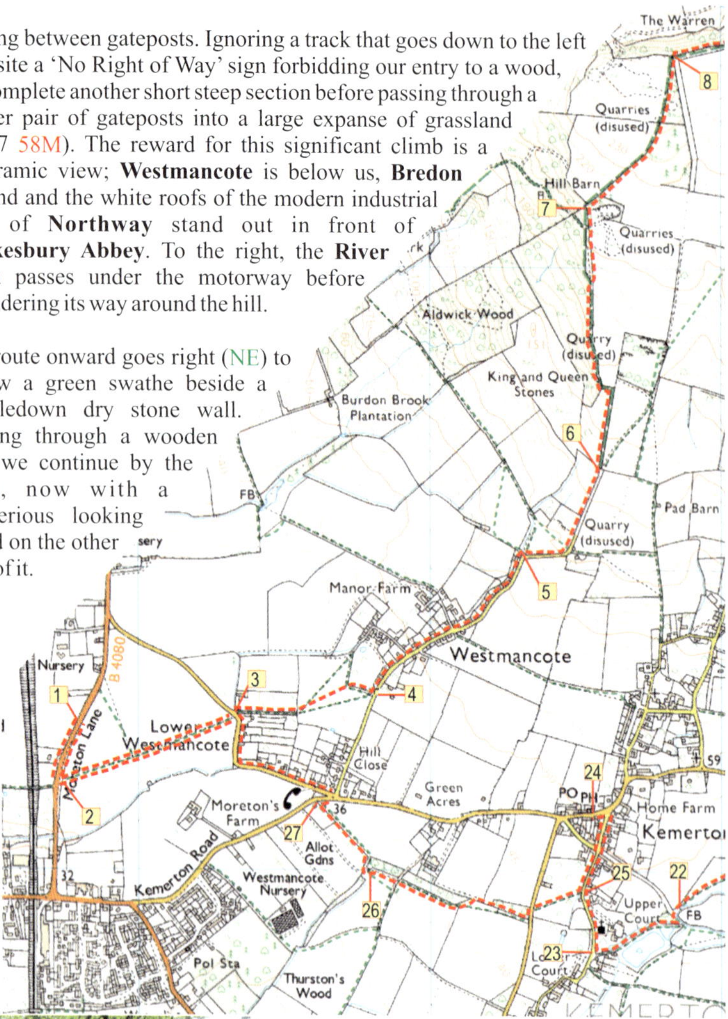

'What tree is that?'

At the next gate (Wp.8 67M) we go right (ENE) to walk between mature trees.

There's the choice of walking straight along the fence that bounds the wood, but our way is through the wood with another dry stone wall preventing sheep falling over the scarp slope beyond it. Ignoring a path down to the left (Walk 4 comes up this way from **Woollas Hall**), we continue though this ancient woodland until a wooden gate takes us into farmland (Wp.9 75M).

Now it's along a wide path beside a well-maintained dry stone wall where we can

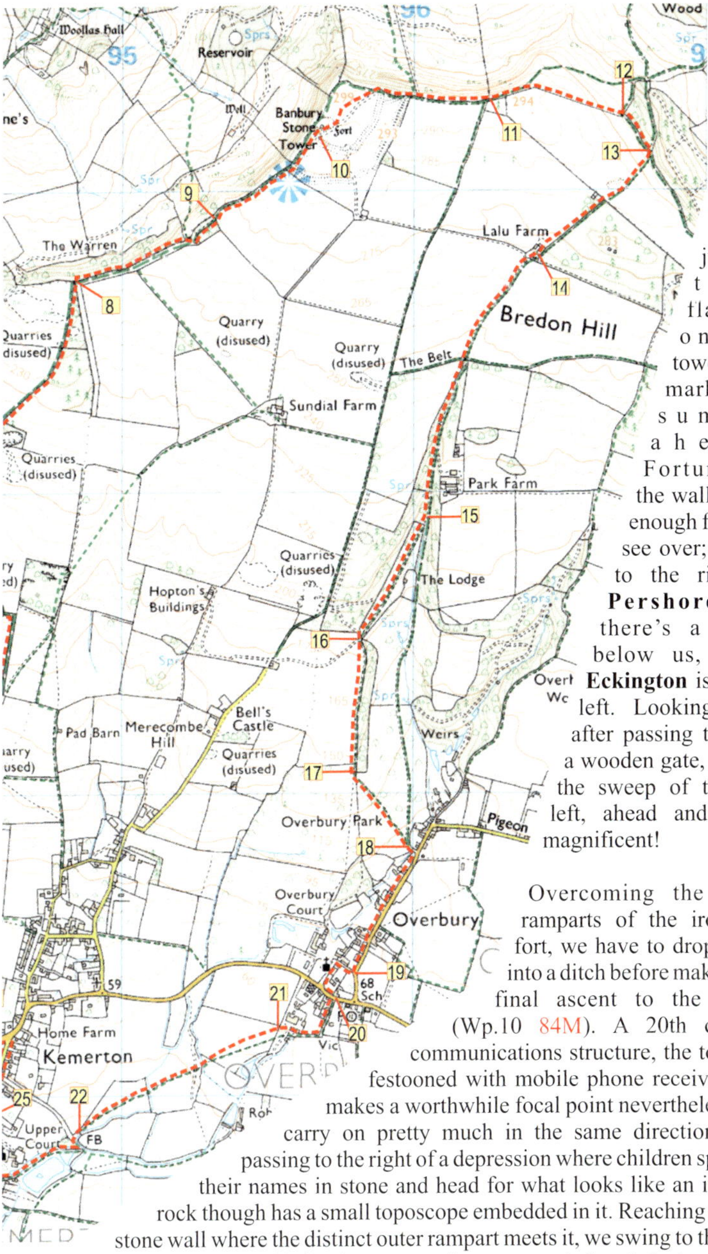

just see the flagpole on the tower that marks the summit ahead. Fortunately the wall is low enough for us to see over; a little to the right is **Pershore** and there's a wood below us, while **Eckington** is to our left. Looking back after passing through a wooden gate, we see the sweep of the hill left, ahead and right; magnificent!

Overcoming the outer ramparts of the iron age fort, we have to drop down into a ditch before making the final ascent to the tower (Wp.10 84M). A 20th century communications structure, the tower is festooned with mobile phone receivers but makes a worthwhile focal point nevertheless. We carry on pretty much in the same direction (NE) passing to the right of a depression where children spell out their names in stone and head for what looks like an isolated rock though has a small toposcope embedded in it. Reaching the dry stone wall where the distinct outer rampart meets it, we swing to the right (E) and carry along with the dry stone wall now to our left and glorious views over it. Next it's through a wooden barred gate (Wp.11 95M) and beside a copse for a short while, then with a fence to our right but now nothing restricting our view to the left; the sprawl ahead is **Evesham** while the village down to our left is **Elmley Castle**. Meeting a larger wood, we go through a wooden five-barred gate (Wp.12 102M) to continue along beside it (SE) with a fence bounding a field to our right. So far, the way since the tower has been flat or gently down but immediately after a path joins up from the left out of the woods (Wp.13 104M) we turn right through a wooden gate (SW) for a short, steady climb up a field. After passing a depression on the right we reach another wooden barred gate and begin our descent. We pass a further copse to our right, then reach **Lalu Farm** (Wp.14 112M) and go right through a wooden barred gate into their yard, then left out of it down a tarmac farm track.

After crossing another track, our way is steadily down through woodland with daffodils, primroses and celandines all around us in spring. Then after ignoring a track up to the left we leave the tarmac (Wp.15 126M) to fork right along a track with a row of fruit trees to its right. Presented with a padlocked gate (Wp.16 136M), we climb over the fence to the left of it then turn immediately left (S) down the edge of a field; what a perfect, placid, rural landscape! A pheasant-filled wood is to our left as we approach another wooden barred gate that takes us into an immaculate field with older trees interspersed with younger ones protected by neat wooden paling; all the work of **Overbury Estate**.

Down to Overbury

Almost immediately we turn left through another gate following a waymark (Wp.17 143M); the way is not so obvious - though there's a path straight on - but we go diagonally right (SE) following no obvious path across the field towards the houses of **Overbury**. Progressing down the hill, we spot a lane sweeping around to the left by a house and negotiating sheep as we go, make straight for it and join it. We pass through a gate by the side of a cattle grid (Wp.18 148M), cross a stream and turn right into a road (SW), all in quick succession. We pass between elegant houses to our right and a bank of daffodils left to approach the village. Just before meeting the main road, we turn right (Wp.19 155M NW), the imposing gates of **Overbury Hall** facing us and a row of charming cottages to our right, then swing left (SW) in front of the hall. **St Faith's Church** is on our right, its unusual lychgate worth a close look. It's such an attractive village; if it was part of the Cotswolds it would be on the coach tour circuit - good luck for us that it isn't!

St Faith's Church lychgate

At the main road we go left (SE) for a few metres before spotting a wooden signpost on the other side of the road (Wp.20 160M) and follow it (SSW) between stone walls.

After going through a chicane of wooden poles it's grassy under foot; we go to the left of a metal barred gate before swinging right (W), then pass barns on either side and cross a tarmac track to a waymarked gate into a field (Wp.21 164M). There's a pond away to our left but again, though the way across the large field isn't obvious, we follow the direction of the waymark diagonally left (WSW) and eventually spot a waymarked stile on the other side. From there it's a little to the right to another stile, a plank bridge and yet another stile all in close order, then straight across the next field making for a metal barred gate with another wooden bridge three quarters of the way to it.

We go straight across the next field too, this time to a wooden barred gate (Wp.22 177M) where a stile to the right of it takes us into scrubby woodland where almost immediately we turn left (S) to walk beside a stream. After another plank bridge at a T-junction, we turn right (W) and emerge by a kitchen garden to a lake with islands, wildfowl and willows, idyllic for a picnic.

.. a lake with islands, wildfowl and willows ..

Walking along the lake with **Kemerton Court** to our right, we keep to the right of a beech hedge and pass **Mill Cottage** before reaching a lane (Wp.23 184M). Here we turn right (NNW) and pass a church as we head towards the centre of **Kemerton** where we meet a main road at the War Memorial and find 'The Crown' a few steps to our left (Wp.24 192M).

After a beer or two and a substantial sandwich, we retrace our steps towards the church but before reaching it, take a right (Wp.25 197M WSW) through a wooden gate to follow a wooden public footpath sign through an orchard of young fruit trees; on the other side an identical gate takes us into a quiet lane. We turn left on the lane, then almost immediately right through an old metal kissing gate to follow a series of waypoint posts (WNW), initially by horse chestnuts. Next it's between a pair of ancient gate posts, through a new metal barred gate, over a track and down the edge of a field with a wood on our right. After swinging left around the end of this field we turn right through a gate into a wood (Wp.26 209M). Here we follow the path first right then left (NW) to emerge opposite a bus shelter.

Turning right then sharp left, we follow a lane (WNW) with the dwellings of **Lower Westmancote** on the right. It sweeps right (N) by a post box - and suddenly the surroundings are familiar (Wp.3 214M). Turning left (WSW), we follow our outward path beside its regular row of trees back to the road (Wp.2 220M) where we turn right (NNE) to find our car parked in the lay-by where we left it (Wp.1 232M). A really satisfying jaunt.

2 OVERBURY

The ring of villages that surround **Bredon Hill** are a real delight. This walk starts in classically beautiful **Overbury** and makes its way up through parkland to the ridge of **Bredon Hill** where it joins the long distance footpath the **Wychavon Way** before going down to **Ashton under Hill** and a refreshment stop at **The Star**. Then it's through fields around the base of the hill visiting **Grafton** and **Conderton** to return.

Walks 1 and 2 can be combined to form a longer walk that runs the length of the hill, returning through the villages that surround it to the south by taking Walk 1 to Wp.13, then continuing on Walk 2 from its Wp.6 and rejoining Walk 1 at **Overbury**. **The Star** still makes a convenient half-way stop.

Access by car:
From junction 9 of the M5 head towards **Evesham** on the A46 and at traffic lights, turn left onto the B4079 to **Bredon**. At a T-junction in the village, turn sharp right signposted 'Kemerton' and after passing through it enter **Overbury** and park by the church. OS Grid reference : SO 95740 37449 Nearest postcode : GL20 7NY.

Access by bus:
Bus number N°540 runs from **Tewkesbury** to **Evesham**. Alight at **Overbury**, a straightforward public transport option for a change! The bus also runs through **Ashton under Hill** (Wp.13 114M), our lunch stop.

.. a row of tiny cottages ..

From where we've parked beside the church (Wp.1 0M) we go forward and around to the right (SE), passing a row of tiny cottages to reach a T-junction. Here we go left (NE) up an attractive lane, along by a wall with our path separated from the lane by grass; there's some highly desirable properties along here; poking our noses through several gates gains a better view of them. We take a left turn (Wp.2 7M) and cross a cattle grid with a stream burbling beneath to follow a public bridleway sign into beautiful open parkland. Following the tarmac lane as it sweeps right (N) by mature oak and horse chestnut trees, the way is gently upward with sheep hiding in the shade. After another cattle grid the lane

The Overbury Estate

sweeps right to pass a pond with a stream running into it, then left before we cross a third cattle grid (Wp.3 20M) and enter woodland (NNE) by a cottage with a beautifully maintained garden. Our way is now steadily upward with neat grass edges to the lane. First a track joins us from the left, then a tarmac lane from the right before we emerge from the wood and cross a rough track (Wp.4 31M). We climb more gently again (NE), through fields towards a farm, with only a communications mast away to our right spoiling the pastoral view. Entering the garden of **Lalu Farm** - it's too tidy to call it a farmyard - (Wp.5 36M) we follow the public bridleway sign to the right, through a wooden barred gate and up beside the farmhouse to a copse. Pretty much at the top of the ridge now, we look back to enjoy great views to the south before going through a wooden gate into a field of long grass, summer home to a myriad of butterflies. After a depression to our left, we see the view to the north and go first gently, then steadily down towards a wood to reach a wooden gate (Wp.6 43M).

Here we go right (SE) along a well-trodden path beside the wood now on the flat; left would take us to the fort at the top of **Bredon Hill** - not for us today though Walks 1 and 4 go there. Continuing along between brambles we remarked while researching this route that, although a bridleway, we hadn't met any horses - and just at that moment met some cyclists who kindly dismount to let us by. Next we come to a meeting of ways (Wp.7 54M). There is a track to the right and a path left down into the woods, but our route is forward and slightly to the left (E). We are now on the **Wychavon Way**, which we'll follow to **Ashton under Hill**. Cruising along the ridge, there are great views to the right while the path bends gently in that direction (SE), still following the edge of the wood. Then leaving its security (Wp.8 62M), we find ourselves on a grassy track beside a dry stone wall with views ahead all around. Straight ahead is **Alderton Hill** while the town to the left is **Evesham**. Beginning to go gently downhill, we swing to the right (SSE) and after ignoring a path that goes steeply down to our left, turn abruptly right (W) to come to a wooden gate on our left (Wp.9 80M).

Through it, we go steeply down (SE) a grassy path, scattered with rabbit droppings, to meet a track that crosses our path (Wp.10 84M). We go across it and half right down to an unusual metal barred gate which has a walkers' gate within it. Stepping through, we go half left (ESE), steadily down a thistle-filled field, then after a stile in a hawthorn hedge, continue in the same direction down. Over two more stiles, we cross a mown field, now on the flat. On the far side we go down a bank, over a stile and head for a waymark post that points a little to the left and for the first time can see **Ashton under Hill**. Down again to a stile and a cinder track (Wp.11 99M), we ignore the path straight on, instead turning right (S) but soon turn left (SE) and go down some steps. Past a rock, over a stile and past a hollow tree we then aim to the right of a church through a glorious meadow, surrounded by butterflies in season.

Through a kissing gate beside the churchyard (Wp.12 106M E), we reach another and go right by the church and out through its lychgate. The village war memorial is surrounded by picturesque thatched cottages but we're ready now to take our refreshment stop at **The Star** (Wp.13 114M) which we find to the left (N).

After this welcome break, we return to the second kissing gate at the rear of the churchyard (Wp.12 120M) and this time turn left (SW) to go along the bottom of the meadow. A gap in the hedge where a gate used to be takes us into the next field to head diagonally up towards a large house with beautifully manicured gardens, seemingly out of place in this farming environment. Here we go through a metal barred gate and straight across a track into a field where we follow the high hedge to our left. Continuing in the same direction we're now on a grassy track between high hedges; when the left hand hedge disappears, we get a closer view of the wooded **Alderton Hill** before reaching a wooden bridge (Wp.14 130M). Beyond this there's a well-defined path through a field of wheat which takes us to a lane (Wp.15 133M) as it swings around a corner and we follow it into the hamlet of **Grafton**. Turning right (NNW), we pass a telephone box before following around to the left (W). Ignoring an even smaller lane on the right before ours peters out, we continue in the same direction on a grassy track down to a wooden barred gate. Following a sign to 'Conderton', we go along the right hand field edge until it turns right, then strike out to the left on no obvious path towards a waypoint post on the near horizon (Wp.16 143M).

This indicates footpaths straight on and to the right; neither are clear but we take the straight on option, initially by an enclosure, then in the same direction over pasture land. After passing through a metal barred gate (Wp.17 148M), we make towards a stile in front of woods up to our right (Wp.18 151M) and enter the woods, the path now unaccountably well-defined.

Ashton under Hill war memorial

We cross a bridge made of three narrow wooden planks before coming out of the woods and continue in the same direction until we reach a track that crosses our path. The positioning of a stile would lead us to believe that the path is to the left of a hedge but none is apparent, so we ignore the stile and carry on along the right hand side of it.

The grassy track narrows to a path before dropping steadily down to the corner of the field, the edge of which we follow around to the right (NNW) now steadily up. Given the chance, we turn left (W) and find a wooden gate (Wp.19 166M) to go steadily up between fields, then steadily down between scabious and along by a plantation of trees. A metal barred gate takes us into the next field, from which a track by a high stone wall takes us down to a lane (Wp.20 173M) where we go left then immediately right.

At a T-junction of lanes (Wp.21 175M) we take the footpath straight ahead over a stone wall aided by steps, then through a gate into an orchard. Similar steps in another wall take us into another orchard and we spot a waymarked stile ahead. This takes us through another field of wheat, over a stile and into dark trees, where we turn right (N).

.. over a stone wall aided by steps ..

A stile to our left appears to be the way - but just past it, around the end of a hedge (Wp.22 185M W) we find a path along the other side of the hedge. Then, after ignoring another stile to the left, we pass **Overbury Bowling Club** and follow the field edge right then left to meet the lane (Wp.23 191M) on which we started at the beginning of this walk. Left (SW), retracing our footsteps, then right (NW) past the row of tiny cottages takes us back to the church (Wp.1 195M). Stunning!

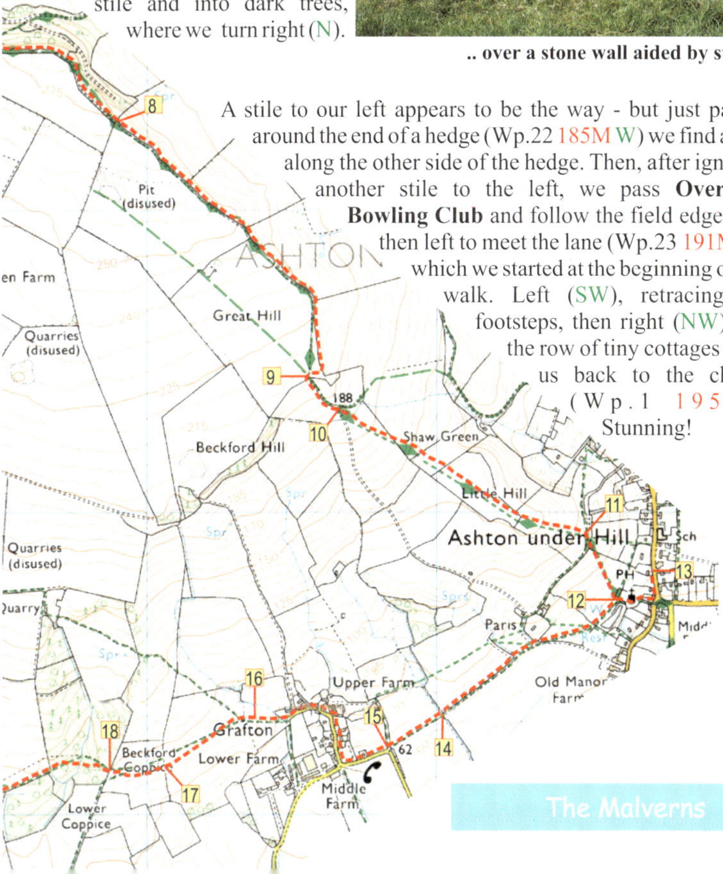

3 ELMLEY CASTLE

Elmley Castle is reputed to be one of the ten prettiest villages in England. This walk takes us up a lane between classic black and white cottages to the ridge of **Bredon Hill** from which (as with Walk 2) it goes down to **Ashton under Hill** and a refreshment stop at **The Star**. Rather than following the well-trodden **Wychavon Way**, we follow a lesser-known route. The way back is entirely on the flat through fields and woodland around the base of the hill, magically arriving back at the start, courtesy of **Elmley Castle**'s mill pond and churchyard.

Access by car:
From junction 7 of the M5 head towards **Pershore** on the B4084. After passing through **Pershore** turn right and then fork left following signs to **Elmley Castle**; there's plenty of space to park on the left opposite the **Queen's Head**. OS Grid reference : SO 98245 41191 Nearest postcode : WR10 3HS.

SHORT WALK OPTION
An attractive much shorter circuit (3.6 miles/5.8km with a similar ascent and descent) would be to simply carry straight on down from Wp.12 to Wp.35.

Access by bus:
There is a bus to **Elmley Castle** from **Evesham** but only once a day so a better option is to catch the Nº540 that runs from **Evesham** to **Tewkesbury** and alight at **Ashton under Hill** (Wp.22 113M) and follow the walk from there.

To start (Wp.1 0M), we continue in the same direction (SSW) up the left hand side of the road alongside a stream that burbles beside us, reminiscent of **Bourton on the Water**. Crossing the road to the pub we decipher 'Elizabeth Queen of' and '1558' from its ancient, fading sign before turning right (WNW) into **Hill Lane**. We walk between picture-book black and white cottages before turning left through a gate into a field after the last cottage on the left (Wp.2 4M). Heeding the 'Please keep to the footpath' sign, we head towards another classic black and white thatched cottage in front of a small hill (W) to find a stile at the edge of the field (Wp.3 6M) and turn left (SW) into a lane and begin to gently climb. After passing the last of a series of magnificent larger properties and at a Public Bridleway sign (Wp.4 14M) the lane degenerates into a steeper, stony track and we're into a wood where bluebells, celandines and primroses abound. At a gate we pass into open fields and shortly come to a meeting of the ways (Wp.5 18M). A track crosses us and though the obvious route seems straight on, we go slightly to the left of this (SW) up a grassy path towards hawthorn trees. At gate posts (Wp.6 24M) our way has been churned up by cows as we continue to a metal barred gate. Rather than going through this we veer half right (W), continuing upward

Up through the wood (after Wp.4)

while keeping a fence on our left. Where a track joins us from the right (Wp.7 29M) we turn left (S) through a wooden gate up into a wood with a poled fence on our left. Another wooden gate (Wp.8 35M) takes us out of the wood. Our climb ends and we turn left (SE) to join Walk 2 to **Overbury**, but not for long! Roots of beech trees reach under the fence to our left, trying to trip us before we reach an open grassy space. Here, Walk 2 carries straight on following the **Wychavon Way** back to **Ashton under Hill** while we go through a wooden gate on the left (Wp.9 47M) to dive steeply down into the wood again (ENE) for an alternative way back to our lunch stop at **The Star**.

.. at the tree we take a right turn ..

The poled fence is still to our left as we reach a couple of signposts (Wp.10 52M) which encourage us to swing left and right as another path crosses us; where our way flattens, there's recent evidence of badgers' excavations. A metal gate (Wp.11 58M) takes us out of the wood into pasture land and on down past a waypoint post, after which the way steepens again. At a second waypoint post (Wp.12 66M) we backtrack right (S) then swing left by a tree to cross a tiny stream (E) and follow a sheep track towards the tree pictured. At the tree (Wp.13 67M) we take a right turn (SE) towards the near horizon with no hint of a path.

Cresting the brow, it's reassuring to spot a metal gate at the left hand end of a hedge and make for it (Wp.14 69M), then go down the left hand side of a field, then a little to the right to cross a stream via stepping stones (Wp.15 71M). It looks as though our route should be through a double gate ahead, but a little beyond and to the right there's a single metal gate (Wp.16 73M) and we go this way instead. Then it's past a water trough, following the left hand field boundary with a newly-made hawthorn hedge before crossing a bridge between gorse bushes (Wp.17 77M).

We now run along the top of a conifer wood, passing a couple of hollow trees, one of which looks as though it's been struck by lightning. Although there are several ways into the wood, we stay on its perimeter, passing through a metal gate and leaping a stream until, eventually, we leave it behind to follow a fence to our left, augmented by hawthorn trees and reach a metal gate (Wp.18 89M). It's tempting to follow the track across the field but our way is along its right hand side (S) by a water trough to its corner where we find a waypoint post (Wp.19 95M). Here we join a boulder-strewn track that drops steeply down to our left (SE) through a rusty, wonky gate to a cattle grid (Wp.20 97M) where we find a farm to our right.

Our track becomes a tarmac lane, first swinging to the left between daffodils and then to the right, continuing steadily down through woodland.

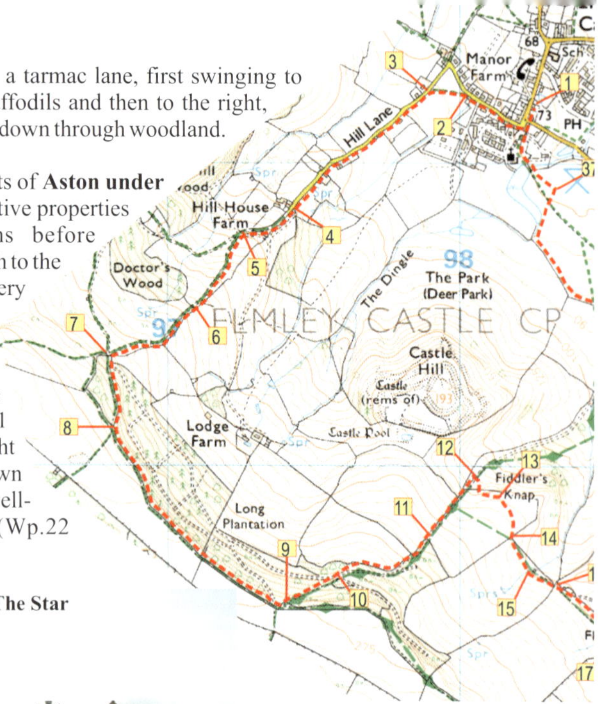

Now on the outskirts of **Aston under Hill**, we pass attractive properties and their gardens before seeking a raised path to the left; the lane is very narrow and there is some local traffic.

As we meet the village road (Wp.21 108M) we turn right (S) and march down to **The Star** for a well-deserved lunch (Wp.22 113M).

The Star

Replenished, we return up the road (N), passing **Cottons Lane** down which we came earlier, then it's left (WNW) into **Wood Lane** (Wp.23 122M) following a wooden public footpath sign.

This residential cul-de-sac quickly sweeps right (N), its surface changing from tarmac to gravel and soon we're on a path that follows the left hand side of a field; the noise from the playground of **Bredon Hill Middle School** away to our right sounds somewhat alien amid this landscape! Next we go over a stile (Wp.24 128M) into a wood, turn left then immediately right (NNW) and carry on through an unusual avenue of flowering trees in a wood. After crossing a track, another stile (Wp.25 131M) takes us out of the wood and along the top of a field. The way is not so obvious now but we follow the edge of the wood into another field (Wp.26 133M) and after crossing that (NW), find a gate (Wp.27 135M) that takes us down steps to a bridge. Then it's up steps the other side to continue left (W) around the wood to a waypoint post where we climb over a metal gate (Wp.28 138M) and turn sharp right (N) along the edge of a field. At its corner (Wp.29 142M) we find a bridge sandwiched between stiles and after traversing that, fork left (NNW) to make our way through scrubby woodland into another field.

Up its left side, we again see a waypoint post (Wp.30 145M) and splash to it through a boggy patch (in damp weather) to find a stile that takes us via more scrub to the next field where the path is thankfully clearer and takes us to a lane (Wp.31 148M).

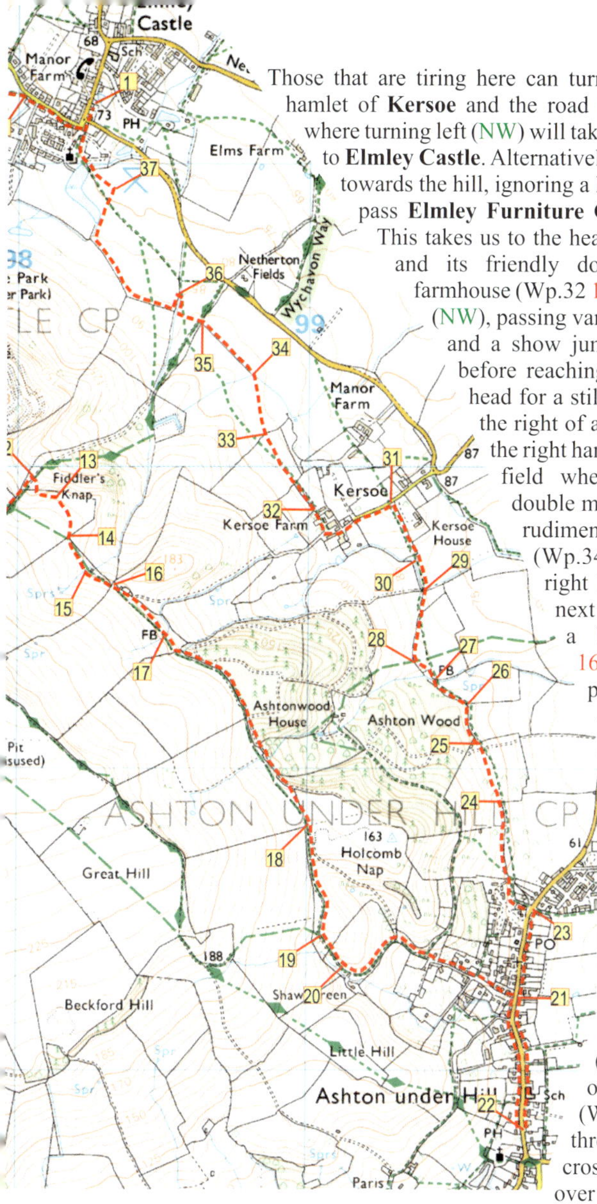

Those that are tiring here can turn right (NE) to the hamlet of **Kersoe** and the road that circles the hill where turning left (NW) will take them straight back to **Elmley Castle**. Alternatively, we turn left (SW) towards the hill, ignoring a lane to our right and pass **Elmley Furniture Gallery** to our left. This takes us to the heart of **Kersoe Farm** and its friendly dogs where, at the farmhouse (Wp.32 152M), we turn right (NW), passing various farm buildings and a show jumping practice ring before reaching a metal gate. We head for a stile (Wp.33 156M) to the right of a metal gate, then to the right hand corner of the next field where to the left of double metal gates we find a rudimentary bridge and stile (Wp.34 160M). At the right hand corner of the next field there's a stile, a bridge (Wp.35 163M) and signposts pointing left, right and straight on; our way is straight on (WNW).

At the field corner we can see our way ahead - but it's on the other side of a stream that may be difficult to cross so we follow its course to the right (N) until we find an overgrown bridge (Wp.36 165M). It's three steps down to the crossing, then up and over a stile - but as our intended footpath has been ploughed over we elect to go around the edge of the field, left then right at both corners until, to the left, we find a stile on its far side (Wp.37 174M).

We enter a different sort of world (NW) where new poled fences separate us from the manicured garden of what might have been the vicarage. The noise of water ahead heralds our arrival at a sludgy mill pond and its mill race, after which the path swings right (NNE) into the graveyard of **St Mary's Church**. We make our way through its attractive lychgate back to the start (Wp.1 180M).

4 WOOLLAS HALL

Woollas Hall

Walks 1,2,3 and 4 all go over **Bredon Hill** too, though this is the easiest way up to the tower at its summit. Starting above the village of **Eckington**, it climbs quite steeply past the elegant 17th century **Woollas Hall**, through parkland, up a sunken lane and along its ridge to the tower.

We return through the quiet, picturesque village of **Bredons Norton** and a lane that runs along the contour half way up the hill. There's a plethora of glorious views.

A SHORTER OPTION

A shorter, but definitely worthwhile option is simply to climb up to the top at Wp.10 and return the same way (2.7 miles/4.4 km) which shouldn't take much more than an hour.

2/3 | 2H 05M | 5.1 miles/8.5km | 370m | 370m | 0*

* though there are two welcoming pubs in **Eckington**

Access by car:

From junction 9 of the M5 head towards **Evesham** on the A46 and at traffic lights, turn left onto the B4079 to **Bredon**. In the village turn left and then right onto the B4080 to **Pershore**. Before reaching **Eckington** turn right, signposted 'Deer Park Business Centre', then right again to **Woollas Hall** and park on the left opposite **Woollas Hall Farm**. OS Grid reference : SO 94583 40939 Nearest postcode : WR10 3DL.

Access by bus:

The best option is to get the N°382 from **Worcester** to **Eckington** where the bus terminates then walk along the road out of the village in the same direction turning left up a lane signposted **Deer Park Business Centre** then right to **Woollas Hall**, a total distance of 2 miles (3.2 km).

An interesting return across the fields would be to follow Wp.18 to Wp.24 of Walk 5, 'Eckington Bridge'.

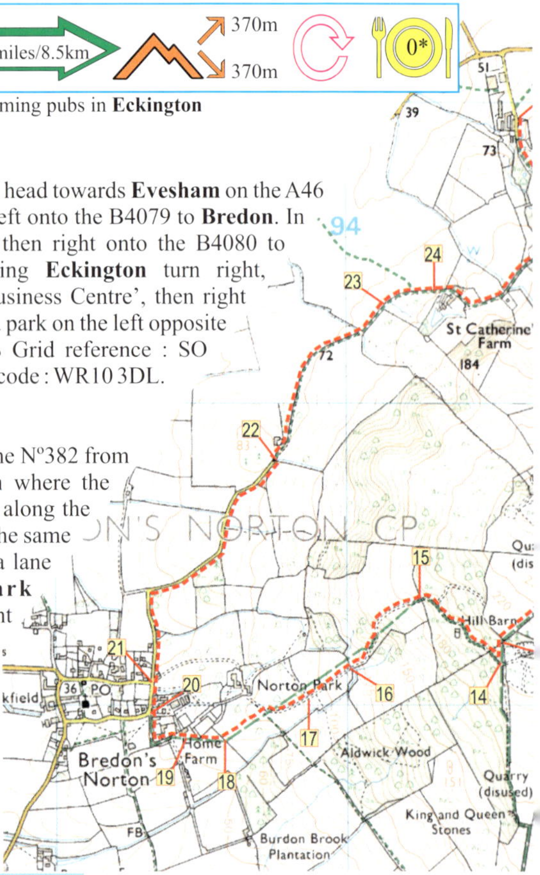

From our car parked opposite the farmhouse (Wp.1 0M), we cross a cattle grid (S) and continue quite steeply up a tarmac lane. Already we can see our objective, the tower at the top of the hill, above us and a little to the left. The lane swings steadily left (SE) then where it sweeps right into **Woollas Hall** (Wp.2 9M) we turn left over a stile and cross a field of sheep (E).

Looking back, the plains that stretch either side of the **River Avon** are already spread out; going forward again, a waypoint post confirms our direction to a stile (Wp.3 14M) where we go right (SE) to join a stony track. After a cattle grid the track becomes boulder-strewn, then where several signs prompt us (Wp.4 17M), we go right to meet a stile to the left of a metal barred gate. Then it's left up the side of a field, following a series of waypoint posts.

.. up a sunken green lane ..

Our clearly defined path swings right (S) by the second waypoint post and we head for the corner of the field to exit it over a stile (Wp.5 24M). Here a track crosses us but we go straight on up a sunken green lane, clearly an ancient way up the hill. Now almost at the end of the steep part of our climb, we swing left (E) before coming to an unusual metal gate incorporating a stile (Wp.6 29M).

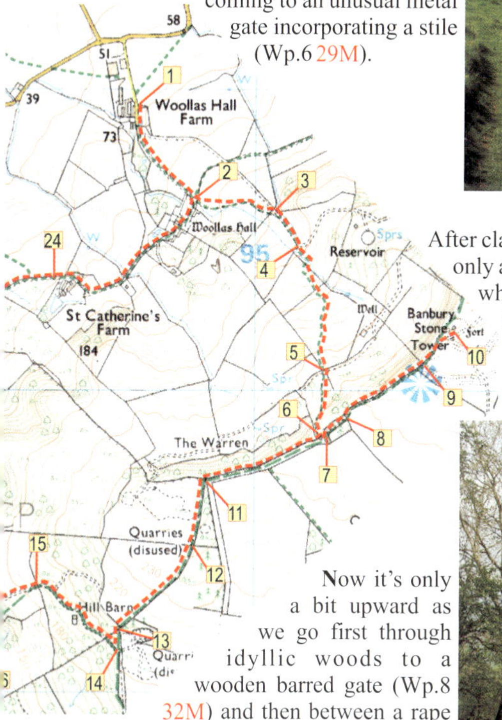

After clambering awkwardly over, it's only a few steps up to the main path which runs along the ridge (Wp.7 30M); here we turn left (NE) to join Walk 1 which comes up from **Westmancote**.

Now it's only a bit upward as we go first through idyllic woods to a wooden barred gate (Wp.8 32M) and then between a rape field and a beautifully maintained dry stone wall with fabulous views down to the left, to reach another wooden gate (Wp.9 36M).

The view from the ridge

Iron age earthworks surround the tower in front of us (Wp.10 38M) which though of no historical significance being a twentieth century communications structure, it nevertheless makes a splendid focal point and a useful windbreak! After retracing our footsteps (SW) along the ridge to where we came up the sunken lane (Wp.7 45M) we carry straight on (ESE) enjoying the view down to the right. Where there's a choice of ways, either will do though we choose the winding path through the wood to the right where at times we have views through the trees down to both left and right.

Eventually we come to a wooden gate (Wp.11 51M) which takes us out of the wood and to the left (S) through a field where a different view opens up to our right across to the **Malvern Hills**. The poorly maintained dry stone wall we pass to our left encloses a mysterious looking wood, then after another wooden gate (Wp.12 54M) we swing steadily to our right (SW) to even more expansive views; what a fabulous walk!

At the corner of this field it's through a wooden gate (Wp.13 59M) and left a bit (S) to go steeply down a rough track. Soon, opposite a gate with a prominent 'Please Keep Out. No Right of Way' sign (Wp.14 61M) we go sharp right (NW) onto another track, now going only gently down, through an area of tussocky grass and a few mature trees. Reaching a metal gate signed 'No Right of Way for Shoot' (Wp.15 65M) we take in the fantastic view with **Bredons Norton** below us before making our way down the steep track (WSW) in front of us.

The track swings left, becoming stony while passing between hawthorn trees then heads right again before a wooden gate (Wp.16 72M) takes us into the next field. Here the track follows a fence on the left, its cinder surface not such good walking for us. Then it's steadily down to a metal gate (Wp.17 75M) after which **Norton Park**, now select holiday accommodation, hoves into view on the right and we pass a couple of beech trees almost overcome with mistletoe.

A track to the right heads to the big house, while our way to the left is confirmed by a waypoint post. After a further metal gate (Wp.18 80M) we follow the track around to the right (W), circling the grounds of **Norton Park**, to a heavy metal gate (Wp.19 82M) and **Home Farm**. Past the farm, we find ourselves beside a dry stone wall which surrounds a house.

Bredons Norton Manor House

The track changes to tarmac and turns right (N) towards **Bredons Norton Manor House** where we can peer through its iron railings. Behind us, the constant rumble of the M5 reverberates in the distance; it doesn't feel part of our world although paradoxically, may have helped bring us here.

We continue straight on through this charming village. A larger lane joins us from the left (Wp.20 86M), then we pass **Meadows Farm Shop** on the right and the larger lane disappears again to the left (Wp.21 88M) all in short order and we are left wandering along a quiet lane. After passing a few houses dotted along it and the prestigious entrance to **Norton Park**, the lane swings right (NE). After a wood to the right from which cacophonous birdsong assaults our ears, we meet the first of many cattle grids (Wp.22 99M).

Again, there are great views as we traverse the track, now stony, through the parkland surrounding **Bredon Hill**

Since reaching the village the way has been relatively flat, but after the next cattle grid (Wp.23 107M) we begin to gently climb and swing to the right (E). At a further cattle grid (Wp.24 109M) we're in the grounds of a modern house built in classical style; two more cattle grids, then we pass a cottage with a 'witch on her broomstick' weather vane, then ultra high fences either side indicate a venison farm and we spot deer grazing some way away to our left.

A magnificent spreading chestnut tree and scrunchy gravel underfoot heralds our approach to **Woollas Hall**, now separated into many individual residential units, the reason why there are so many cars about. After a gate and yet another cattle grid we are back on tarmac (Wp.2 119M) and go steeply down (NW) back to our car (Wp.1 125M).

5 ECKINGTON BRIDGE

This beautiful walk explores the part of the Avon where it runs around **Bredon Hill**, visiting the villages of **Birlingham**, **Great Comberton** and **Eckington** and climbing the lower slopes of the hill to enjoy the view across its valley.

A SHORTER VERSION

A shorter version (6.7 miles/10.7 km) heads directly back along the road to our starting point (pavement or footpath all the way) after the pub stop (Wp.24) rather than taking the prettier way back along the river. An easier way still is to take the N°382 bus from outside **The Bell**!

Access by car:

From junction 9 of the M5 head towards **Evesham** on the A46 and at traffic lights, turn left onto the B4079 to **Bredon**. In the village turn left and then right onto the B4080 to **Pershore**. After passing through the village of **Eckington** we drop down to traffic lights that control single file traffic over **Eckington Bridge** and turn right immediately before them into a car park by the river. OS Grid reference : SO 92241 42252 Nearest postcode : WR10 3DD.

Access by bus:

Bus number N°382 from **Worcester**; ask the driver to drop you off at **Eckington Bridge**.

Eckington Bridge

From the car park (Wp.1 0M), we take time to admire the picturesque 16th century **Eckington Bridge** before crossing it (NNE), ever mindful of the traffic, stopping half way across in a niche to look along the river. On the other side we turn right off the road and pass through a metal kissing gate (Wp.2 3M).

Although the obvious path is beside the river, our way is to the left (ENE) across a stunningly green field, testament to how often it gets flooded, with **Bredon Hill** ahead and to the right of us. Reaching abundant cow parsley at the edge of the field we go through another metal kissing gate (Wp.3 13M) and turn right to join a path (ESE) that almost immediately joins a grassy track running beside a ditch and an avenue of trees. At a T-junction of tracks (Wp.4 15M) we turn left (N) beside a cereal crop, then at a further T-junction (Wp.5 17M) head right (E) towards nicely converted farm buildings on the perimeter of **Birlingham**. Meeting a lane (Wp.6 20M), we turn right (S) and circle **Birlingham Manor House** following the lane left (ESE), then left again (NE) until we come upon a lane on our right (Wp.7 23M).

We follow it (ESE) between a tiny mail box on a post and a beautiful thatched cottage - what magnificent views up to **Bredon Hill** the properties along here must have! Ignoring a lane on the left, we carry on (SE) past a 'No Through Road' sign. As we leave the village the lane degenerates into a track running between cow parsley and hawthorn hedges. On reaching a field, we keep to its right-hand edge and begin to hear the sound of water.

A path to our right (Wp.8 35M SW) takes us through trees towards a weir; now the water crashes with such force it drowns out all other sound! After crossing the weir, we reach the relative calm of **Nafford Lock** where a bridge (rather than the more usual perilous journey across the top of lock gates), takes us on to a second massive weir structure, recently constructed to help control the regular flooding of **Tewkesbury** and **Gloucester**.

Leaving the river, we climb steadily up, ignoring a track on the right and instead take a narrow footpath up by a cottage with its beautifully landscaped garden. A lane (Wp.9 43M) marks the end of our short climb. We turn left (E), then shortly after where the lane swings right, carry straight on over a stile and into a field. The well-defined path leads us between a cereal crop and parallel to **Bredon Hill** and towards the village of **Great Comberton**, its church tower just visible. Towards the other side of the field we go gently down into a gully to cross a wooden footbridge (Wp.10 52M). In the next field, deer graze nervously; their forebears must have escaped when venison was farmed locally.

After crossing another gully, we follow along between a hedge and a fence to a metal kissing gate where a tree has been struck by lightning (Wp.11 57M). This leads to a delightful field which, when crossed diagonally but still continuing in the same general direction, takes us to a stile to the right of a metal gate (Wp.12 61M). Crossing the stile is tricky - watch out for your rucksack getting entangled with a tree - then we cross a wooden bridge and follow a wooden fence on our left (ENE) gently up towards a large red house.

.. copious buttercups and daisies ..

Beside the house, we cross a stile to the right of a metal barred gate to reach a road (Wp.13 66M) where we turn right (SE) with copious buttercups and daisies fronting **Great Comberton Church**.

The road swings right and steadily descends (SSW), leaving the village. At the bottom of a dip where the road goes further right and just after the entry to a track (Wp.14 70M), a wooden footpath sign leads us across a stile and steadily up (SSE) beside a field edge.

At the top of this first field we walk beside a gully before reaching a stile (Wp.15 76M), then it's further up (SE) beside mature oak trees to another stile with a waymark encouraging us to climb even further.

At last, where keeping straight on up would have required the skills of mountain goats, we turn right (Wp.16 83M) to follow a flat grassy track (WSW) with **Bredon Hill** ridge just above us. The going is much easier so we can now enjoy the views forward to the **Malvern Hills** and down to the right of **Eckington**, **Birlingham** and **Great Comberton** with **Pershore** behind them.

After passing a pond to our right surrounded by stinging nettles and another to our left, this time enclosed by a barbed wire fence, we reach a stile to the left of a metal barred gate, our track now rocky and an electric fence to the right. Another stile by a gate takes us to a gate by a water trough (Wp.17 97M) where we cross a flinty track to follow the left field edge. The going is now grassy again as we swing a wee bit left (SSW) to reach **Woollas Hall** (Wp.18 100M), the centre of attention for Walk 4.

Here we turn right (NW) and it's steadily down a tarmac track to **Woollas Farm** where we go over a cattle grid and the track becomes a lane. The outbuildings of the farm have been converted to **Deer Park Business Centre**, a very attractive, well landscaped development and we remark on an avenue of young horse chestnut trees to our right which, no doubt, will last longer than any of us! At a T-junction (Wp.19 110M) we turn left (W) onto a busier road and ignore the signposted lane on the right to 'Eckington' as our way there is across fields. Soon we follow a wooden footpath sign protruding from the hedge (Wp.20 113M) to go through a metal kissing gate and head diagonally left (WNW) across a field.

Our path veers right when it reaches the other side and we go along the bank of a stream until we reach a path to the left, almost hidden by brambles but nonetheless easily passable, that takes us across a recently replaced bridge (Wp.21 120M). The path continues diagonally right across several fields separated by hedges. First there's a gate-sized gap, then a narrow gap with a half dismantled stile and here we

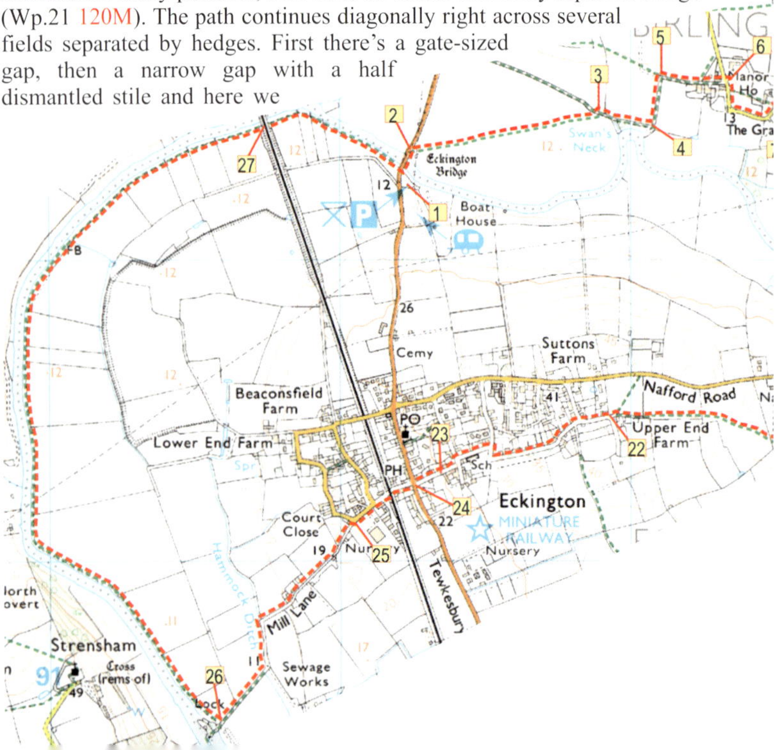

nudge left (W) to go along a field edge and then between buildings to pop out by a bend in a lane (Wp.22 132M) on the outskirts of the village.

Joining another lane that swings in from the right, we continue in the same direction between well-groomed properties of varying ages, then swing right immediately before turning left into **School Lane** to pass between school and village hall. After jinking left and right through an angled crossroads, we reach **The Anchor** on our right (Wp.23 140M) and adjourn to the bar, the first refreshment opportunity we come to in the village. After a well-deserved break, we continue down the lane to reach the main road (Wp.24 142M) and **The Bell**; the shorter version of this walk goes to the right, to go back to the bridge along the road. It's a pleasanter choice than it may sound, as once out of the village, the way is along a path protected from the road by a hedge.

Cruising on the Avon

For the more stalwart, however, it's straight across the main road (WSW) to a metal footbridge over a railway - a sleek Virgin train hurtles beneath us (while researching), whisking bodies between north and south-west, our world and theirs seeming totally divorced.

Now in the quiet residential **Station Road**, the name a reminder of a pre-Beeching era when **Eckington** and **Bredon** both had stations, we ignore a road on the right, then carry straight on where our road swings right (Wp.25

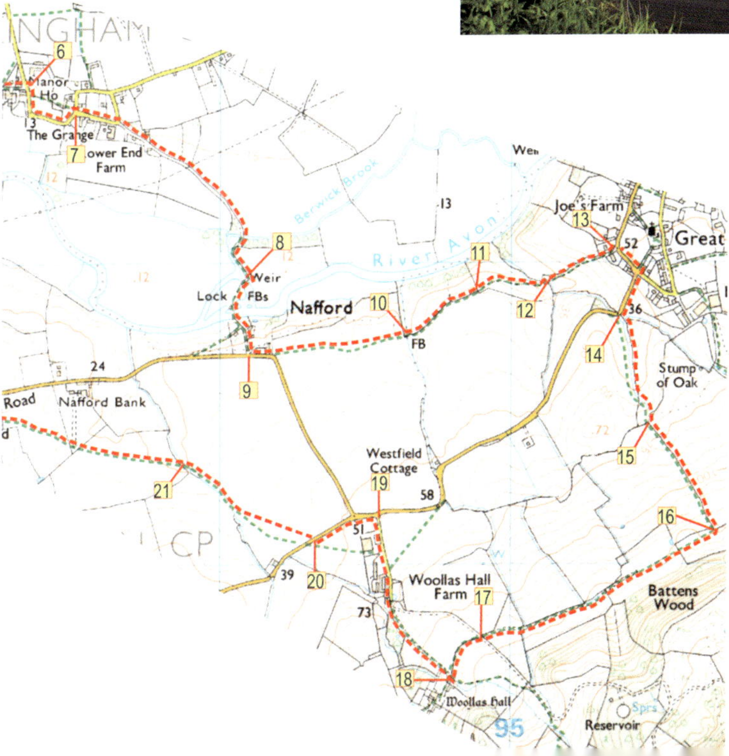

where our road swings right (Wp.25 145M SW) into **Mill Lane** whose road sign helpfully adds 'To the River'.

Looking forward, it's difficult to believe that the church we can see is on the other side of the river as we swing left and right past **Court End Farm** and go gently down to reach the flat, alluvial flood plain. After passing a camp site we reach **Strensham Lock** (Wp.26 157M) where we turn right (NW) through the first of a series of metal kissing gates. We soon pass permanent moorings on the left to enjoy abundant flower bedecked meadows. The river turns right through a full 180º as we follow it from **Strensham Lock** back to **Eckington Bridge** as narrow boats and cruisers pass by.

Bredon Hill, from beside the Avon

A sailing club and further moorings bear witness to the amount of leisure activity on the river before we reach a railway bridge (Wp.27 191M ENE).

As we approach **Eckington Bridge** we see **Bredon Hill** ahead again. Eventually **Eckington Bridge** hoves into sight again and after a final kissing gate, we cross the road back to the car park (Wp.1 202M).

6 PERSHORE BRIDGE AND TIDDESLEY WOOD

This easy walk runs along beside the river Avon, then through **Tiddesley Wood** before returning to explore **Pershore Abbey**. A quick loop into the town demonstrates how successful the planning department of the council has been in maintaining its character and there's an unusually varied choice of refreshment opportunities as well. Return to **Pershore Bridge** is through the abbey grounds and then by footpaths.

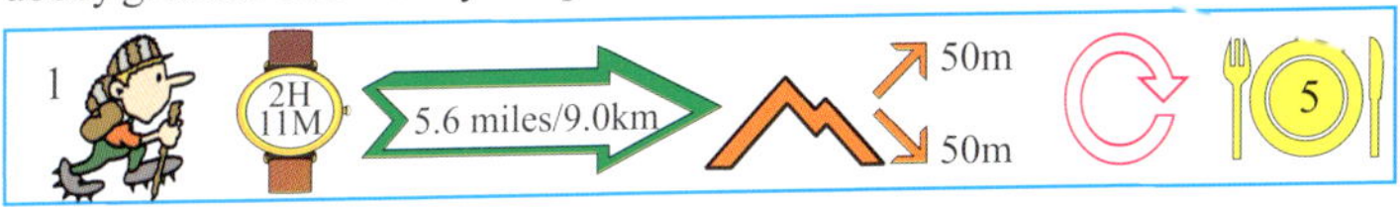

Access by car:
From junction 7 of the M5 head to **Pershore** on the B4084 and go straight through this busy town; soon after leaving the town we cross the **River Avon**, parking immediately after it on the left in the **Pershore Bridge** car park. OS Grid reference : SO 95246 45081 Nearest postcode : WR10 1AS.

Access by bus or train:
Bus number N°550 from **Worcester** goes as far as **The Star** in **Pershore**, continuing for a short distance in the same direction to the start of the walk at **Pershore Bridge**. Though you could take the train to **Pershore Station**, unfortunately it is way out of town and the necessary walk is not one to be savoured.

Old Pershore Bridge

Before leaving the car park (Wp.1 0M) it's worth pausing at the various information boards; it's interesting that when a new concrete road bridge was built in 1926, the original stone bridge dating from 1413 was left for pedestrians - other towns take note!

Heading across it (WNW), with busy traffic on the new bridge to our left and the odd narrow boat or cabin cruiser passing below, we come to the main road.

Crossing with caution, we go to the left beside black railings with water meadows the other side until we reach a kissing gate (Wp.2 3M). Through it and down some steps takes us beside the water and between cow parsley and buttercups, to follow the 'Pershore Bridges Circular Walk'; at least to start with. The well-worn path takes us through a metal gate with the river now below us and cow parsley six feet (2 metres) tall. Our path swings right (W) and after passing woodland, we cross a bridge (Wp.3 15M) over a tiny tributary, no more than a ditch really. A field of rape lies to the right between us and modern housing, while in the other direction **Bredon Hill** hogs the skyline.

Swans glide on the river

On reaching a track we turn left to carry on close to the river. At a second wooden bridge we ignore a path to the right to continue along the river, looking out for swans gliding by using their wings as sails.

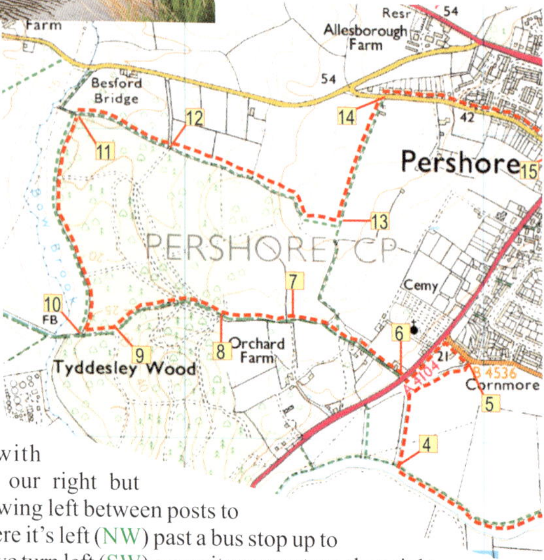

With **Pershore Abbey** now visible above the buildings surrounding it, we approach another wooden bridge, this time enclosed by metal gates (Wp.4 28M).

We turn right (N), up the left hand edge of a field by a ditch. The path turns right around the corner of the field (ENE) with **Bredon Hill** now to our right but given the chance, we swing left between posts to a road (Wp.5 34M). Here it's left (NW) past a bus stop up to **Defford Road** where we turn left (SW) opposite a cemetery, then right opposite a nursery (Wp.6 38M), following a 'Public Bridleway' sign up a tarmac lane (WNW).

After passing several attractive properties we reach the end of the lane where we go to the right of a picture-book thatched cottage and through a gate - to be presented with a luxuriant field but no sign of which way to go! Carrying on in the same general direction we make for the far right hand corner where we find a stile (Wp.7 44M) to take us (W) into an adjoining field. We keep to the left hand field edge by a ditch towards **Tiddesley Wood Nature Reserve** which we enter over a stile to the right of a gate (Wp.8 47M).

There are many paths through this wood; first we take the rightmost of the two alternatives, then after crossing a track we fork right onto a relatively minor path which could be a little muddy. We wander through varied woodland accompanied by a cacophony of birdsong to reach a crossroad of paths (Wp.9 54M).

Going straight on again, we reach the edge of the wood (Wp.10 57M) where we turn right (N) over a stile, into a field of buttercups and daisies with pastoral views across open countryside. Following the wood's edge and with **Bow Brook** down to our left, we go over a stile into a plum orchard; as

Pershore Purple is a popular plum variety, perhaps these are they. At the wood's corner (Wp.11 69M) we follow it around to the right (ESE) to join a footpath just inside it.

The plum orchard beside Tiddesley Wood

Where a track crosses us (Wp.12 75M), we go through a metal gate and are out in the field again where rabbits gambol undeterred by our presence between newly planted trees. After two more metal gates we're fenced in on both sides; it's steadily up with a whiff of garlic carrying to us from the wood, still to the right.

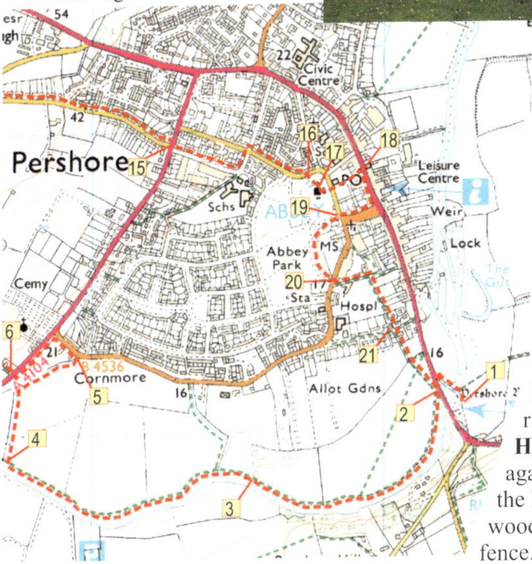

Following the 'Public Footpath' sign to the right and with **Bredon Hill** appearing before us again, we head around to the left and away from the wood beside a barbed wire fence.

At a T-junction of paths (Wp.13 85M) we turn left (NE) to walk along a grassy track; the going underfoot becomes gravel as we approach a road (Wp.14 91M).

Turning right (E), we pass by 1930s housing as we head steadily down back to the town. Reaching a main road (Wp.15 99M) it's right then immediately left into **New Road** - such unimaginative road naming - and by business units towards **Pershore Abbey** tower. After the road swings left (NNE), we turn right opposite the **Victoria Hotel** (ESE) and pass attractive timbered buildings before reaching a mini-roundabout. Here it's left to go through a single black metal gate on the right (Wp.16 105M) into the grounds of **Pershore Abbey** where an avenue of ancient beech trees lead us to its entrance (Wp.17 107M).

After exploring the interior of the small and thoroughly charming abbey, we turn left out of the entrance to pass under buttresses (SSE), then left again (ENE) around it to pass out of the grounds through a gate and across a road to **St. Andrew's Parish Centre**.

Passing to the right of it, we find the garden here a haven of tranquillity. A 'Happy Face' sculpture and modern wrought iron gates lead us past **Pershore Heritage Centre** to emerge into the bustle of **Pershore High Street** (Wp.18 111M) where we turn right (SSE) to be presented with a tempting choice of refreshment opportunities.

.. Happy Face ..

Sugar'n Spice is a traditional tea room behind a cake shop where each table is given the name of a local village. Then there's **Number Eight**, a more upmarket coffee shop fronting **Number Eight Arts Centre** or **The Angel**, a dark oak coaching inn on the other side of the road are all recommended.

Pershore Abbey

Turning right again (WSW) into **Market Street**, we progress to its opposite end then act as if we're going right but spot a way forward between stone walls back into the abbey grounds (Wp.19 115M).

Along a tarmac path with mature trees spaced between cut grass, this is another totally serene area. **Pershore Abbey** is to our right as we fork left towards a colourful children's playground, then it's left again (SSE), continuing to swing left through an avenue of ancient oaks and elegant black lamp-posts.

Emerging between stone walls (Wp.20 120M), we cross a road and head along a public footpath by **Pershore and District Sports Club** (E) until, faced with a brick wall, we turn right (SE) to circle the sports ground and emerge at the end of a residential road (Wp.21 124M).

Here it's straight on between houses, ignoring the path to the left, to go over a stile behind them, back into the water meadows that bound the **Avon**. Our way is straight on rather than the more obvious path to the right, through long grass towards the bridge where the steps leading up to a black kissing gate (Wp.2 128M) are familiar. We retrace our steps along our outward path, left then acutely right to cross **Old Pershore Bridge**, back to our car (Wp.1 131M).

7 THE SEVERN AND THE AVON

Almost two thirds of this walk follows river banks so no climbing is involved; choose a sunny weekend to watch the English at play on the water. It starts right by the motorway but dives straight into woodland, then it's across fields to the attractive village of **Ripple** and down lanes to the **River Severn** and on to **Tewkesbury** where a turn around **Tewkesbury Abbey** is recommended before lunch; return is beside the **River Avon** to **The Fleet Inn** at **Twyning** where a further refreshment stop is surely justifiable, before getting back to the start with a view of **Twyning Manor** on the way.

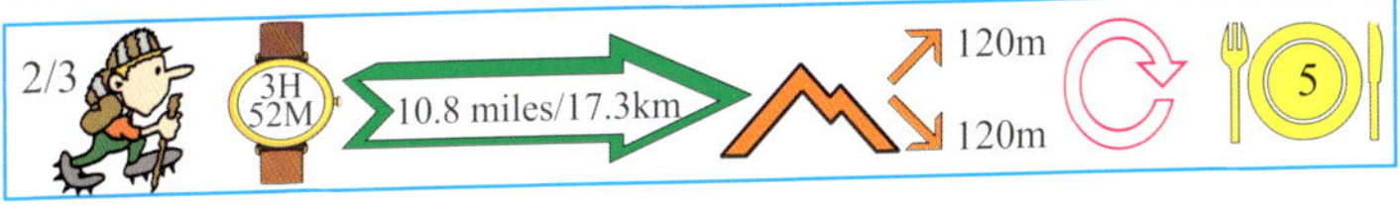

Access by car:
This must be the walk starting nearest a motorway junction. From Junction 1 of the M50 we take the A38 north towards **Worcester** and park in the lay-by immediately on the left. OS Grid reference : SO 88685 37743 Nearest postcode : GL20 6HG.

Access by bus:
Buses N°s 362 and 363 go from **Great Malvern** to **Upton on Severn** then, from the same bus stop, N°351 takes us to the start of the walk on its way to **Tewkesbury** and **Gloucester**; ask for the motorway junction.

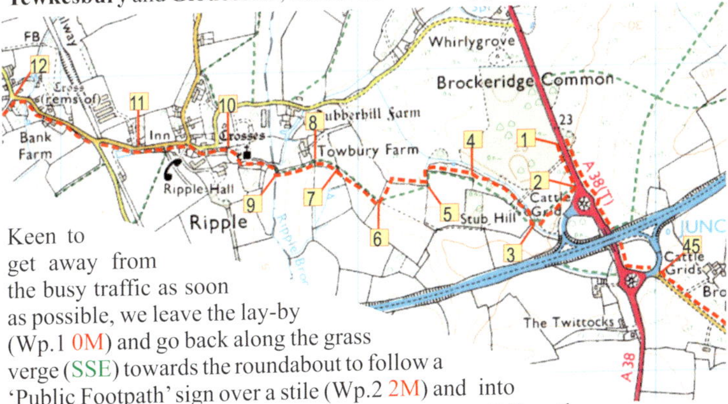

Keen to get away from the busy traffic as soon as possible, we leave the lay-by (Wp.1 0M) and go back along the grass verge (SSE) towards the roundabout to follow a 'Public Footpath' sign over a stile (Wp.2 2M) and into a wood. Aided by a waypoint tacked to a tree, we follow the winding path (SW) between bluebells to a wooden bridge and decrepit stile (Wp.3 6M) where we go right (NW), following the wood's perimeter. A series of waypoint posts mark our route, with blackberry bushes abounding, then left of a crab-apple tree we spot a waypoint post by a gap in a hedge (Wp.4 11M) to go into a field with the church at **Ripple** straight ahead.

A stile on the far side is clearly our way (WSW), but this field is in cultivation so we go around its right hand perimeter to reach our objective (Wp.5 13M). It's exactly the same for the second field (Wp.6 16M) though we can go straight across the third field (NW) towards a thatched farmhouse. Getting closer, we see, head for and cross a stile (Wp.7 20M) to find an orchard. Making for a log store, we then go slightly left (WNW) up to another stile (Wp.8 22M). Next it's along by the kitchen garden of the farmhouse (WSW),

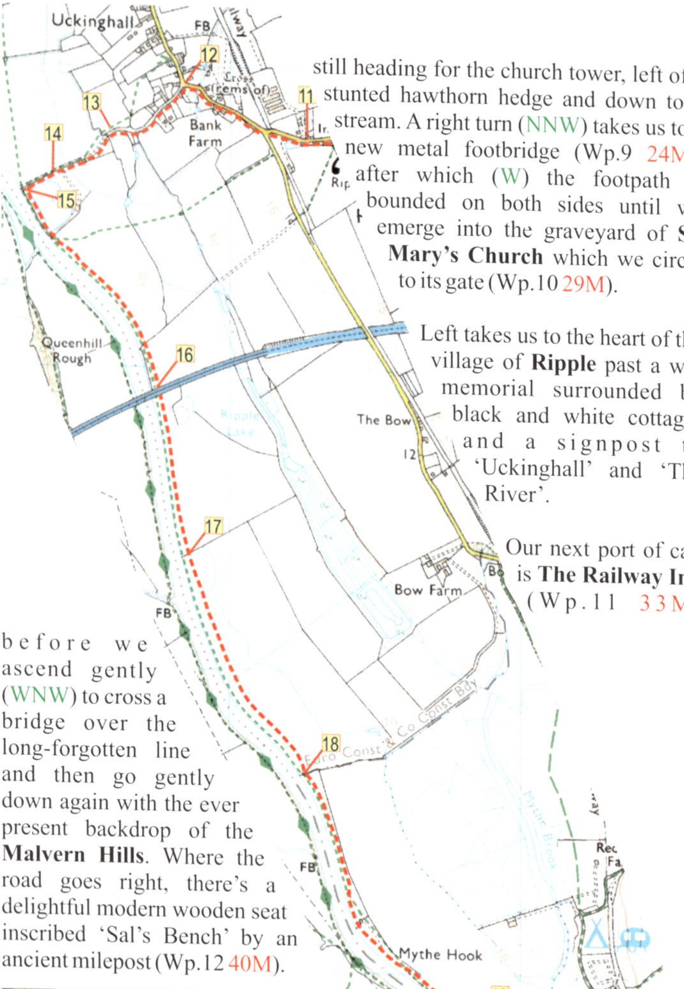

still heading for the church tower, left of a stunted hawthorn hedge and down to a stream. A right turn (NNW) takes us to a new metal footbridge (Wp.9 24M), after which (W) the footpath is bounded on both sides until we emerge into the graveyard of **St. Mary's Church** which we circle to its gate (Wp.10 29M).

Left takes us to the heart of the village of **Ripple** past a war memorial surrounded by black and white cottages and a signpost to 'Uckinghall' and 'The River'.

Our next port of call is **The Railway Inn** (Wp.11 33M) before we ascend gently (WNW) to cross a bridge over the long-forgotten line and then go gently down again with the ever present backdrop of the **Malvern Hills**. Where the road goes right, there's a delightful modern wooden seat inscribed 'Sal's Bench' by an ancient milepost (Wp.12 40M).

Sal's Bench

We go left (SW) along **Ferry Lane** through a landscape that clearly floods regularly, first on a tarmac lane, then at a cattle grid (Wp.13 45M) it becomes a stony, potholed track, then later, after a car park for anglers, grass appears down its middle and finally we go right between fences (Wp.14 48M) as instructed by a sign erected by the owners of houses ahead.

Passing in front of them to a stile (Wp.15 50M), we reach the **River Severn** and turn left (SE) along its bank. After further houses we pass under the motorway bridge carrying the M50 (Wp.16 62M) and shortly after, duck beneath a conveyor belt that carries quarried sand to a waiting barge; as this is a public right of way we assume it's passed the rigours of Health and Safety! A barbed wire fence appears to block our way (Wp.17 72M) so we move a little to the right to find a stile amongst stinging nettles.

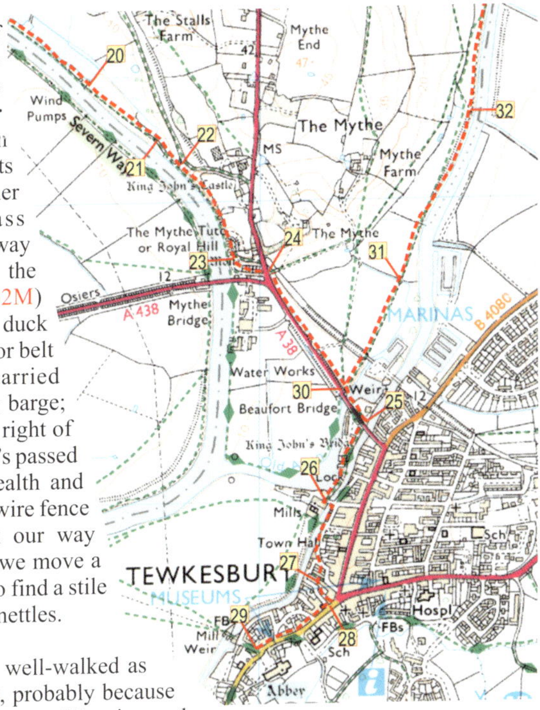

The path isn't as well-walked as you might expect, probably because the alternative **Severn Way** is on the other side of the river. You could continue through the long grass but it's easier to walk further left, by the field's edge. At the next field boundary we again move right to find a stile closer to the river (Wp.18 82M), this time continuing along beside the water with **Tewkesbury Abbey** just in view. After a stile to the left of a wooden gate (Wp.19 97M) we come to an embankment between the river and a lake, a gentle area of cow parsley, hawthorn and mature trees. Soon though, at a further stile (Wp.20 108M), we pass out of it into a field. At its far side (Wp.21 112M) we naturally join a track that crosses a substantial bridge over a tributary of the river.

Mill Avon

As the track swings left (Wp.22 113M), we follow a footpath straight on through woodland until, after negotiating a landslip, we see a busy road bridge crossing the river ahead; here our journey beside this river comes to an end (Wp.23 120M). We go left (E) up a track that becomes a tarmac lane before reaching the main A38 road (Wp.24 122M) where we turn right (SE) and head towards **Tewkesbury**, carefully negotiating the junction with the A438. After crossing the **River Avon**, we go down steps (Wp.25 129M) following a 'Severn Way' sign and pass narrow boats (SSE) moored by modern mews houses on the **Mill Avon**.

This smaller watercourse, separated from the main flow by the frequently flooded **Severn Ham**, supplies water to the old wooden water mill, just as its name suggests. After hopping over lock gates, we reach a giant Victorian mill (Wp.26 134M) and go left over a bridge, then immediately right along quaintly named **Back of Avon** road. After it moves away from the river (S) we fork right and after a car park turn left onto a footpath signposted 'Abbey and Town Centre' curiously described as 'Post Office Lane' (Wp.27 138M).

Suddenly emerging into the noise and bustle of the town (Wp.28 140M), we turn right (SW) to pass **John Moore's Countryside Museum** on our way to **Tewkesbury Abbey** (Wp.29 145M). There are lots of places to eat here; a good choice is the **Hop Pole Inn**, relaxing by the river before retracing our route back to the steps from the bridge (Wp.25 157M). (An alternative return is to continue to **The Cross**, go left along the **High Street** and left at the mini-roundabout by **The Black Bear**, reputedly Gloucestershire's oldest pub.)

Tewkesbury Abbey

Where the Avon joins the Severn

Back on route, we cross the road and go left (NW), then right immediately after the bridge (Wp.30 159M) to follow a green 'Public Footpath' sign down steps to a stile. Across a field (NNE), we fork right heading for another defunct railway bridge, the weir and lock gates where the **River Avon** joins the **River Severn** to our right. After going under the railway bridge we come to a bridge over a ditch and a stile (Wp.31 165M).

There's a plethora of boats in a marina - if they all emerged at once, the boat jam would resemble the M25! Next it's a gaggle of sailing boats around a sailing club and at the second stile (Wp.32 171M), the yellow of the rape crop (in season) on **Bredon Hill** shining brightly in the sun. After the next stile **Twyning Church** is visible to our left, then following a further stile (Wp.33 178M) the river swings right; we see the spire of **Bredon Church** straight ahead - as it's on the far side of the river it's a fair assumption that the river must swing back left again - and so it does. A concrete bridge between wooden stiles (Wp.34 185M) takes us on (N), with a kayak centre on the opposite bank and a motorway bridge far ahead but, before reaching it, we go through a metal gate (Wp.35 195M) and a poled fence separates us from the river with a grand Georgian house to our left.

A gate to the right of a barred gate and a narrow bridge takes us to **The Fleet Inn** (Wp.36 198M) and a welcome drink. We could take the road that runs down to the river back through **Twyning** (WNW) and straight up to Wp.44 but we go right (Wp.37 199M NNE) along a lane behind the pub, a caravan site on our left and attractive cottages to the

Twyning Manor

right. The lane swings left (WNW) before we reach a junction (Wp.38 202M) and go right into a larger lane signposted 'Strensham'. After passing a right fork we turn left (Wp.39 206M W) onto a muddy track just after a farm building, climbing gently between hedges.

At a meeting of ways (Wp.40 209M) it's straight on over a stile and up a footpath backing onto residential properties. At a further stile we ignore the right hand option to go straight on up the left side of a field.

Presented with more options (Wp.41 212M), we go right and left onto a smaller path (NW) still along the back of properties, down a bank to a road (Wp.42 214M). Crossing and turning left (SW), we soon see a tarmac path to go up and right between posts (WSW) onto a gravel footpath. On reaching the end of a cul-de-sac, we find a kissing gate on the right (Wp.43 216M).

Though the obvious path runs beside willows, we go left (W) with **Twyning Manor** ahead and right. The way isn't that clear but we head for a metal water trough, then around the left hand edge of a field. Skirting a pond, we join a tarmac lane that takes us away from the manor towards its lodge where we negotiate an unusual stone stile to the left of a cattle grid. On meeting a road (Wp.44 226M), we go right (NW) until we reach a larger cattle grid and a T-junction (Wp.45 226M). Crossing the road, we turn left, following a roundabout around to the right, then it's under a motorway bridge and around another roundabout to our car in the lay-by on the far side of the road (Wp.1 232M).

8 ODDA'S CHAPEL

Apperley Church

This gentle stroll along the **River Severn** takes in three interesting but very different ecclesiastical buildings and three riverside pubs. Starting in **Apperley**'s unusual church, it follows an attractive lane to **Deerhurst** where the **Priory Church** and **Odda's Chapel** both date from Saxon times, then follows the river to **Haw Bridge** before returning through woodland.

Access by car:
From junction 9 of the M5, we take the A438 towards **Tewkesbury** and follow the bypass around the town to pick up the A38 to **Gloucester**. Turning right at traffic lights onto the B4213 signposted 'Apperley' and 'Tirley', then right into the village of **Apperley**, we turn left and fork right by the war memorial to park by the church. OS Grid reference : SO 86119 28070 Nearest postcode : GL19 4DQ.

Access by bus:
Buses N°362 or 363 go from **Great Malvern** to **Upton on Severn** then, from the same bus stop, number N°351 goes via **Tewkesbury** to **Apperley** on its way to **Gloucester**.

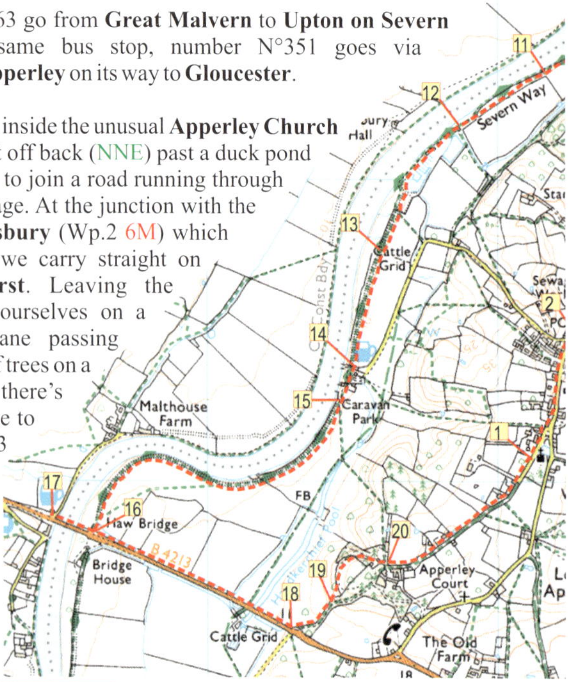

After taking a look inside the unusual **Apperley Church** (Wp.1 0M), we set off back (NNE) past a duck pond and war memorial to join a road running through this attractive village. At the junction with the road from **Tewkesbury** (Wp.2 6M) which brought us here, we carry straight on towards **Deerhurst**. Leaving the village, we find ourselves on a pleasant, quiet lane passing through a funnel of trees on a ridge. Before long there's a metal barred gate to the left (Wp.3 11M) offering fabulous views across to the **Malvern Hills**; the view to the right's not bad either!

Through an incongruous modern flood gate (Wp.4 28M), we pass **Deerhurst Manor House** and swing left, another lane joining us from the right. At a junction (Wp.5 30M) we turn left (NW) and follow a signpost to 'Odda's Chapel' and 'Deerhurst Church' and turning right (N) through a metal gate to visit the first of them (Wp.6 33M). A Saxon Minster dating from c.800AD, it's vastly different in style from the church at **Apperley**. After a look inside, we follow the building around to the right and go down steps to gaze upward at 'The Angel', a carving high up on the exterior wall (Wp.7 37M).

The inscription in Odda's Chapel

Back at Wp.6, we continue to the right (NW) and then around to the left (SW), passing **Abbot's Court** before reaching **Odda's Chapel** (Wp.8 43M), restored by English Heritage to its original state.

An inscription on the wall tells us that the chapel was built in 1056AD by Odda, kinsman of Edward the Confessor, in memory of his father.

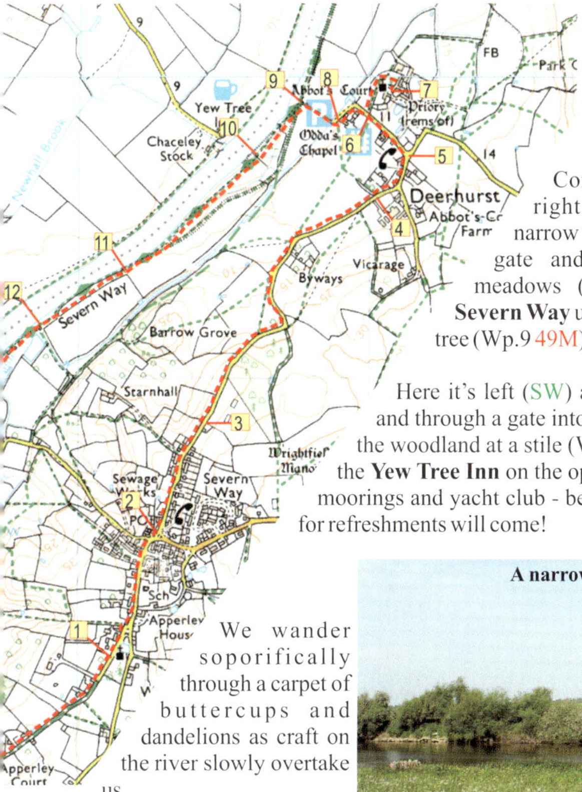

Continuing, we turn right, pass through a narrow gap to the left of a gate and go across water meadows (NW) to meet the **Severn Way** under a spreading oak tree (Wp.9 49M).

Here it's left (SW) along the river bank and through a gate into woodland. Leaving the woodland at a stile (Wp.10 53M) we spot the **Yew Tree Inn** on the opposite bank with its moorings and yacht club - be reassured, our time for refreshments will come!

We wander soporifically through a carpet of buttercups and dandelions as craft on the river slowly overtake us.

A narrow boat on the Severn

After a stile (Wp.11 61M) hidden in a hedge to the right of a metal barred gate we're in shoulder-high cow parsley, then at a further stile (Wp.12 66M) we're in woodland again before passing a property bounded by leylandii.

Where the path divides, we take the right hand fork to stay close to the river and reach a stile to the left of a metal gate (Wp.13 73M) which takes us back into water meadows. Patience is rewarded as we arrive at **The Coalhouse Inn** (Wp.14 79M) - ice cold cider is recommended, while relaxing on a bench right by the river.

Rested, we carry straight on through a gap between houses and caravans but are soon out of this populated place as a stile (Wp.15 82M) takes us back into water meadows. The path swings slowly right (W) through the next field, then left again (SW) before reaching a stile to the left of a metal gate (Wp.16 98M) and a road. Turning right, we cross the **River Severn** over **Haw Bridge** (WNW), enjoying the view back down the river.

Haw Bridge Inn

It's a pleasant surprise to find two hostelries (Wp.17 102M): the **Riverside Inn** on the right and the **Haw Bridge Inn** on the left. It would be unfair not to try them both! After imbibing we return across the bridge (ESE) and carry on up the ruler-straight road, raised above the land either side. Clearly it often floods as a number of stagnant pools remain.

Soon after a bridleway crosses the road, we reach the 50mph signs for **Lower Apperley** and at a lay-by on the left (Wp.18 114M), follow a footpath into a wood (NE). We ascend gently between bluebells until we reach a metal gate (Wp.19 116M) where the footpath has been diverted to the left. After a further metal gate, we go right and then suddenly climb steeply, but not for long as soon we emerge into a gorgeous buttercup meadow where the path gently swings right (E) before joining the concrete of **Apperley Court Farm** (Wp.20 121M). A quick right and left takes us into a quiet lime tree-lined lane (NE) back to **Apperley Church** and our car (Wp.1 129M).

9 UPTON UPON SEVERN

Based around the picturesque riverside town of **Upton upon Severn**, this gentle stroll starts out along the river following the **Severn Way** then crosses the ham - a local word for the pasture land that gets flooded almost every year - to the **Drum and Monkey** at **Newbridge Green** (closed Monday lunchtime). Return is across fields to **Upton** and its plethora of opportunities to while away the rest of the day.

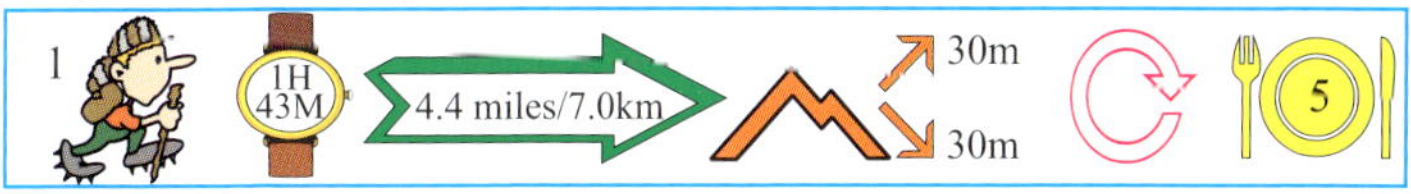

Access by car:
From junction 1 of the M50 head towards **Worcester** on the A38 then turn left onto the A4104 towards **Upton upon Severn**. After crossing the river turn left at a roundabout to head into town - but where the main road turns right, turn left to go beside the river passing the **King's Head** and **The Swan**, parking on the left. If there's no space along the river, one can usually be found in one of the adjoining side streets. OS Grid reference: SO 85360 40661 nearest postcode WR8 0JD.

Access by bus:
Bus Nº 362 or 363 runs every 30 minutes from **Great Malvern** to **Upton on Severn** but note there are none on Sundays.

From the river bank where we've parked the car (Wp.1 0M), we continue along the road (ESE) between willows on the left and grand houses on the right with an attractive, arched pedestrian bridge over the entrance to a marina on the opposite side of the river. Where the road ends, we follow a footpath to the left of a metal barred gate by a 'Severn Way' signpost and then go through a wooden gate to walk beside the ham.

.. a tiny beach

To the left, the river beyond the scrubland is glimpsed only intermittently, while to the right is this vast expanse of green field as flat as a billiard table. After the river begins to swing gently right (SE) a post with '1' on it (Wp.2 13M) marks steps left and down to the river, where we find a tiny beach between two fishing platforms, a good place to sit and watch the boats go by. Back on the path, we continue to swing right (S) and pass several fishing pitches, each with wooden steps built down to individual platforms. Opposite substantial waterworks we look to the right and back

Across the ham to Upton and the Malverns

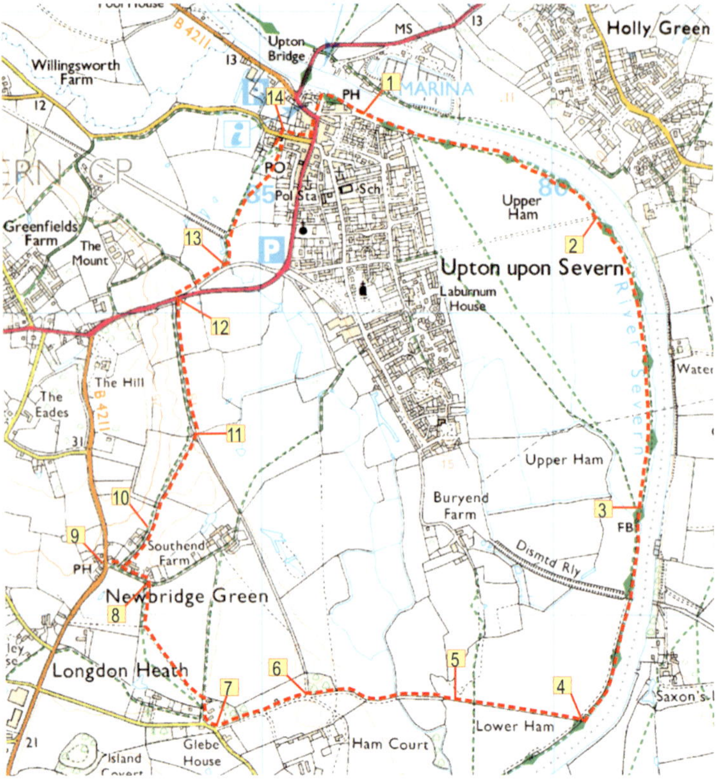

across the ham to **Upton upon Severn** and beyond the town to **The Malverns**.

Eventually reaching the edge of this vast field (Wp.3 27M), we go through a metal gate into a further field. Now we're closer to the river and notice large arrows on poles planted in the river to ensure that traffic keep well away from its banks. Next it's through another metal gate with the embankment on our right - the sole reminder of the bridge carrying the long-dismantled **Malvern** to **Cheltenham Spa** railway line.

After a wooden stile (Wp.4 37M), we turn right away from the river (W) following faint wheel tracks along the right hand field edge. Then at the corner of the field, a metal barred gate (Wp.5 43M) takes us onto a track between hedges which swings left and right while gently climbing, the only noticeable gradient of the day. After a spinney on our right we carry straight on at a crossroad of tracks (Wp.6 50M WSW) with beautiful, thoroughbred horses grazing on both sides behind wooden fences. Passing through an open metal barred gate, we reach a lane at **Glebe House** (Wp.7 54M) and turn right (WNW), then after only a few steps go right again (N) signposted 'Close Cottage'.

A few steps further on a wooden signpost points left while green metal ones point straight on and half left. Our way is half left (NW) over a stile by a metal barred gate, there is no sign of a path but we make for a gap in the hedge on the other side of the field. Reaching this, and finding it to be an open gate we turn right (N) and follow along this side of the hedge. A stile takes us to a narrow path between claustrophobically high hedges, but before long we reach a lane (Wp.8 65M) and turn left (WNW). We pass more desirable properties and a lane to the right to reach a larger road where we find the **Drum and Monkey** almost opposite (Wp.9 68M).

Re-crossing the road, we retrace our steps, this time going left (NE) along the lane we passed earlier. After an open gate with a stile beside it, the track is gravel-surfaced; we leave it courtesy of a stile on the right (Wp.10 72M) to find ourselves on a grass path, an avenue of trees separating us from farm buildings. After another stile we're back on a track with a church steeple visible between trees straight in front of us until, after an open metal barred gate, the track disappears and we go along the right hand edge of a field with **Bredon Hill** on our right. In the corner of the field we could go down a bank to a rusty barred gate but it's better to go straight on over a stile where a path takes us to a metal gate and onto a substantial track (Wp.11 77M).

Left (N) along this track with **Upton** away to our right takes us through a wooden gate by a lodge to cross a busy road (Wp.12 84M). We go right (E) on the pavement then when confronted by a rowing boat full of flowers, almost immediately turn left down the old road to **Upton**, a new road built as this one was often impassable due to flooding. We ignore the first public footpath to the left and follow the second through a black painted kissing gate (Wp.13 87M), down a track (NE), and across playing fields with the embankment to the left another reminder of the dismantled railway. Aiming for the right hand corner of the playing fields, we go to the right of tennis courts, around a children's playground and into a pay and display car park (Wp.14 96M).

Upton upon Severn

We head right (E) into **New Street**, past the **Bell House Café** and left (N) in the centre of the town by the old coaching inns of **White Lion** and **Talbot Head** hotels.

Where the main road goes left we get a fine view of the **Pepperpot**, an old church tower now serving as a heritage centre telling the story of the town through the ages. Here we go straight on turning right (ESE) by the **King's Head** where at the time of researching, a surprisingly large pleasure boat was moored on **The Severn**, and follow the river bank past **The Swan** back to where we parked the car (Wp.1 103M). There's plenty of interest nearby to while away the rest of the day.

The Pepperpot

10 WORCESTER AND THE SEVERN

From **The Swan** at **Martin Hussingtree**, we head west to find the recently restored **Droitwich Canal** at **Ladywood** then follow it through glorious countryside to where the canal joins the **River Severn**. The remainder of the walk follows the river bank to the heart of historic **Worcester**, finishing with **Riverside Walk**, a splendid avenue of beech trees beside **Pitchcroft Racecourse**. We finish at the bus station to catch one of the frequent buses (except for Sundays when they run hourly) back to the start.

Walks 10 and 11 can be neatly combined to form a circular walk starting from **Martin Hussingtree** with a lunch stop in **Worcester**. Continue straight on at the bridge just after Wp.34 to connect up with Wp.2 of Walk 11.

Access by car:
From junction 6 of the M5 head towards **Droitwich** on the A4538, described as 'A38' at an unhelpfully signed roundabout. At traffic lights in **Martin Hussingtree**, go right onto the A38 and immediately right again into the car park of **The Swan**. OS Grid reference: SO 88327 60194 Nearest postcode: WR3 8TY.

The Swan

Access by bus:
Take bus Nº 44, 44A, 44B or 45 from **Great Malvern** to **Worcester Bus Station** then Nº 144 or 244 to **Martin Hussingtree**. The walk ends at the bus station, ideal for getting back.

Leaving our car in the neatly hedged car park of **The Swan** (Wp.1 0M), we cross the main road at traffic lights and disappear down **Drury Lane** (NW) opposite, leaving the noise of the A38 behind. Where the lane swings right (Wp.2 4M) we go straight on though a gate to the left of a metal barred

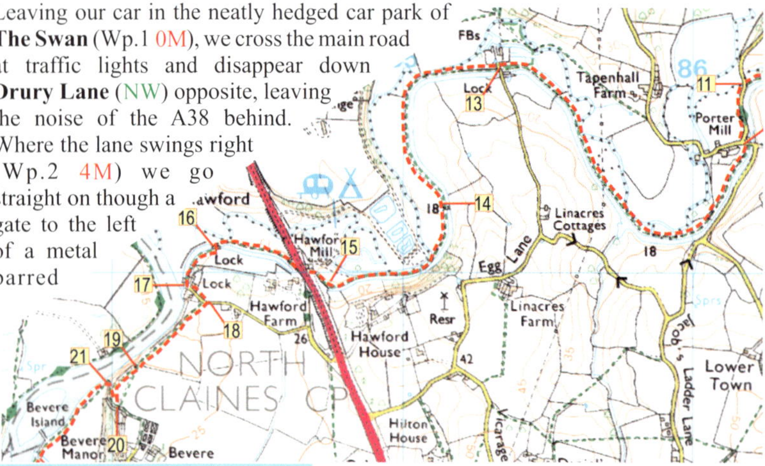

gate and immediately left over a stile.

Then it's diagonally right though long grass to another stile and behind a low wooden building by a fence. Although thc way doesn't seem well-trodden so far, things soon improve. A stile in the fence (Wp.3 7M) takes us into a field; following around its edge, we ignore a gap into the next one and instead, a mite further on, find a further stile (Wp.4 9M). Diagonally crossing the large expanse before us, we make for its far corner; there doesn't appear to be a way out until a stile appears as we near it (Wp.5 12M).

Steps take us down to a bridge, over a stream and half-right to a rusty metal gate tied up with string; we climb over it and then go left (W) up the side of a field to its corner. There, after two stiles in quick succession (Wp.6 15M), we carefully cross a railway line. A stile the other side takes us between a cereal crop to another stile. Houses come into view on the skyline, then a further stile takes us into a field of horse boxes and farm machinery; we head down its right-hand side to a heavy gate (Wp.7 20M) leading onto a lane; we head right (N) into the outskirts of **Ladywood** where the lane swings left (NW).

Reaching a junction (Wp.8 26M), we turn left (W) signposted 'Porters Mill' and 'Hadley'. After passing a footpath on the left, we cross the **Droitwich Canal** (Wp.9 32M) and turn left (SW) to stroll along its tow path. It's worth taking a few minutes to laze on a conveniently positioned bench by the first lock to admire the quality of its recent restoration.

A restored lock gate on the Droitwich Canal

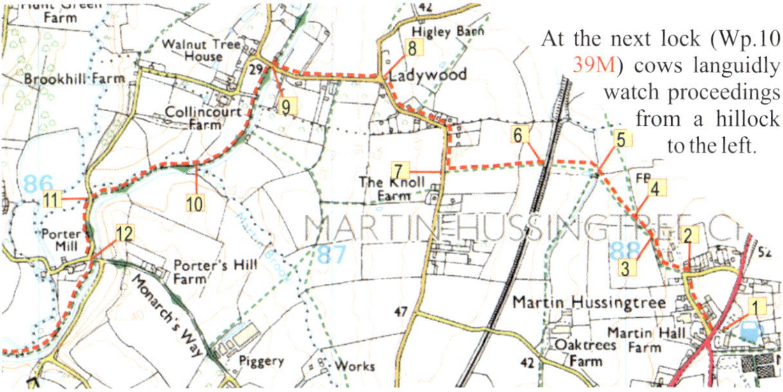

At the next lock (Wp.10 39M) cows languidly watch proceedings from a hillock to the left.

A little further on, where a lane runs close to the canal (Wp.11 44M S), another bench is in a prime position to study a swan's nest secreted in bullrushes on the opposite bank. Where the lane begins to swing to the right behind a house, it seems that our way is leaving the canal but on reaching a T junction (Wp.12 48M) we go left and then right (SW) by a public footpath sign, continuing our journey along the right hand side of the canal. In this serene environment, with the **River Salwarpe** in close attendance though rarely making its presence obvious, the canal gently swings a full 90º to the right (NW), following the contour as it must before reaching a bridge (Wp.13 66M). The canal swings back left (S) to a surprisingly substantial bridge (Wp.14 77M) considering it only carries a farm track, then right (W) where traffic noise from a major road ahead is audible.

Beside the Droitwich Canal

After passing a caravan site behind a viciously spiked metal fence, we pass under the dual carriageway by means of a modern tunnel (Wp.15 84M) enjoying the echoing clank, clank, clanking of our footsteps.

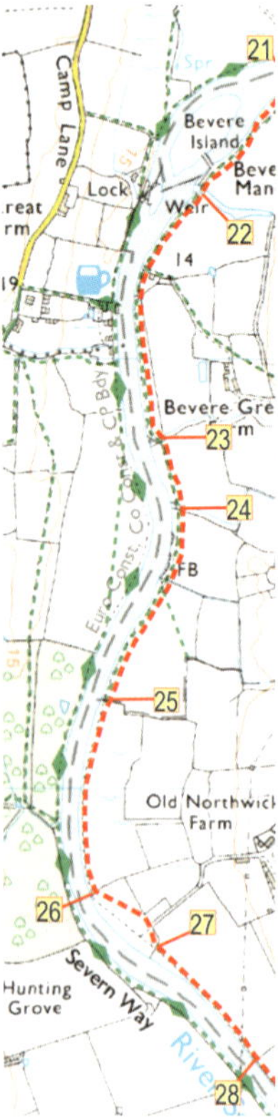

We soon come to a further lock (Wp.16 90M) and cross a bridge just beyond it, so that we're now to the left of the canal and ready to meet the **River Severn**. Swinging left (SW), we arrive at **Hawford Lock** (Wp.17 93M) where the canal ends. Unfortunately there's no further right of way beside the water, so we zigzag steeply up to the left, then less steeply to the right up a scrunchy drive (SE) that links this cluster of sought-after properties to the rest of the world.

After the last house we go sharp right over a stile (Wp.18 94M) and along a grassy path (SW) bounded by a fence to our left with the river just visible through trees but now far below us. After passing a cereal crop it's up a steep bank and over a stile (Wp.19 99M) to carry on along the right-hand side of a field, the shrubbery now so dense to the right that the river is obscured.

As we approach a high brick wall, but before reaching it, we turn right back on ourselves (Wp.20 101M NW) and go steeply down through woods, then left (SW) and over a stile (Wp.21 103M) to find ourselves back close to the river by an enormous motorway-like sign warning craft of the weir ahead. After a kissing gate, it looks as though the substantial bridge ahead crosses the river - but on investigation find that it only takes cows for grazing on **Bevere Island** which sits in the middle of the river between the weir and a lock.

After a gate alongside the weir (Wp.22 108M) we pass between a gravel beach and some pine trees before reaching a wooden gate to the right of a white house.

A glade takes us beside the white house to another gate under a spreading chestnut tree and we're back into an area of long grass again, until a further gate takes us beside a cereal crop. Approaching a hedge, it seems as if we're leaving the river but at the last moment a sharp right turn takes us over a bridge (Wp.23 118M) into a buttercup meadow and then to a bridge sandwiched between metal gates (Wp.24 121M).

A nicely-made information board tells us all about **Northwick Manor Heritage Trail** which we must have stumbled onto, then after a wooden gate (Wp.25 127M), we pass into an area of long grass, cow parsley and buttercups. The presence of more people and dogs indicates we're approaching **Northwick Lido** as we go through a metal gate (Wp.26 133M) into the lido, a large expanse of grass designed as a playground for the city dwellers of **Worcester**.

The main path left (SE) takes us almost to a car park but at a black rubbish bin we go a little to the right towards a metal gate (Wp.27 136M) and into a buttercup-strewn meadow populated by horses. In its corner (Wp.28 141M) our way becomes a narrow well-trodden footpath where we're hemmed in close to the river by a fence hidden in a hedge.

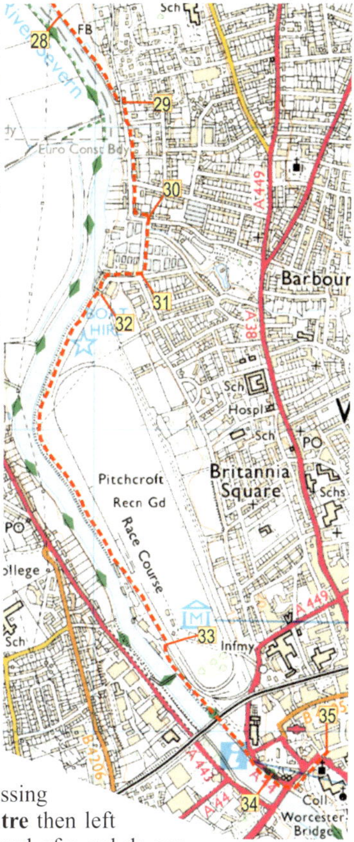

A narrow high bridge takes us over a creek, past a sadly decaying hulk lying on its side, remnant of previous years' floods.

Before long we leave the river again and climb up steps between railings (Wp.29 147M) to go right (S) along a tarmac path behind houses. We soon join an unadopted residential road, encouraged by a sign that 'Pitchcroft' is only three quarters of a mile distant. We head into **Park View Terrace**, a proper tarmac road; soon after it swings left we go right along another tarmac footpath (Wp.30 153M) into **Gheluvelt Park**.

Straight across it, we meet and turn right on a road (Wp.31 155M W), passing the **Pump House Environment Centre** then left (SW) behind terraced houses to the end of a cul-de-sac where a gate (Wp.32 158M) takes us into **Pitchcroft Park**. Turning right, we follow **Riverside Walk**, finding boats for hire from the last house of the terrace.

.. a beautiful avenue of beeches ..

An amble between a beautiful avenue of beeches which runs between the river and the famous **Pitchcroft Racecourse** takes us almost all the way to the city centre. Where the river gently swings to the left (SE) we can admire the splendid houses on the other bank with gardens running right down to the water's edge.

As we approach a boathouse (Wp.33 214M) we move to the right in order to pass between it and the river and, under a footbridge, may meet shoppers returning from the city, laden with carrier bags.

After going under a railway - this time live, well and crossing the river on a Victorian viaduct - we must join the roadside as we approach **Worcester's** only road bridge over **The Severn**. Just before reaching it we cross the road at a pedestrian crossing (Wp.34 218M) and at a corner turn left (NE) into **Bridge Street** to head towards the bus station. Again, we use crossings at the next junction before going left into the Pedestrian Zone where our final way point (Wp.35 221M) is at the entrance to **Crowngate Shopping Centre**.

Our GPS record has to end here as we go to the left and indoors into the alien, air conditioned environment. Straight on and then around to the left, we find an escalator which takes us down to the bus station and from stand 'O' take bus Nº 144 or 244 back to **Martin Hussingtree**.

11 WORCESTER AND ITS CANAL

Another gentle meander, this walk starts in the centre of **Worcester**, first along the **River Severn** and beside its magnificent cathedral then out of the city beside the **Worcester and Birmingham Canal**. After a staircase of locks by **Offerton Farm**, the walk cuts through lanes, fields and woods to **Martin Hussingtree**. A frequent bus service (except for Sundays when it's hourly) takes us back to the city centre.

Walks 10 and 11 can be neatly combined to form a circular walk starting from **Martin Hussingtree** with a lunch stop in **Worcester**. Continue straight on at the bridge just after Wp.34 of walk 10 to connect up with Wp.2 of Walk 11.

Access by car:
The walk starts in the centre of **Worcester** from the bus station. By leaving the car where the walk finishes and bussing to the start, car park charges are avoided. From junction 6 of the M5 head towards **Droitwich** on the A4538, described as 'A38' at an unhelpfully signed roundabout. Go right at traffic lights in **Martin Hussingtree** onto the A38 and immediately right again into **The Swan**'s car park. OS Grid reference: SO 88327 60194 Nearest postcode: WR3 8TY. To the left is a bus stop from where the frequent N°144 or 244 (hourly on Sun) goes into **Worcester**.

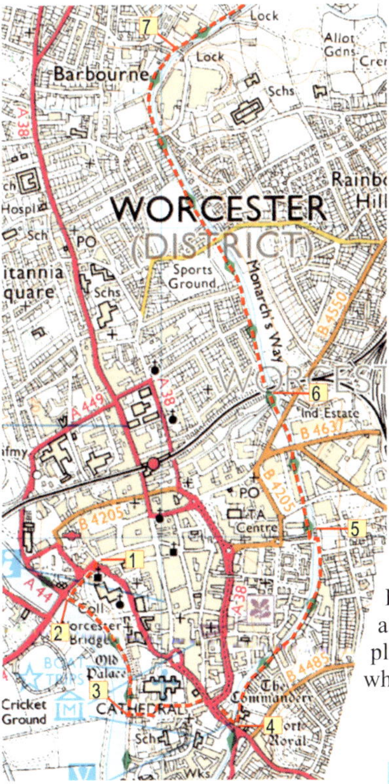

Access by bus:
Take buses N°44, 44A, 44B or 45 from **Great Malvern** to **Worcester Bus Station** where the walk starts.

From the bus station we go via steps or escalators into the heart of **Crowngate Shopping Centre** and turn right past clothing stores to emerge into a pedestrian precinct where GPS tracking can start (Wp.1 0M).

Turning right (S), we head out of the precinct and cross the road facing us at a pedestrian crossing, then follow its left-hand side (SW) down to a bridge over the **River Severn** (Wp.2 3M). Keeping this side of it, we go left (SE) along **Riverside Walk**, perhaps passing armadas of swans or children playing in fountains and a jetty from which boat trips depart.

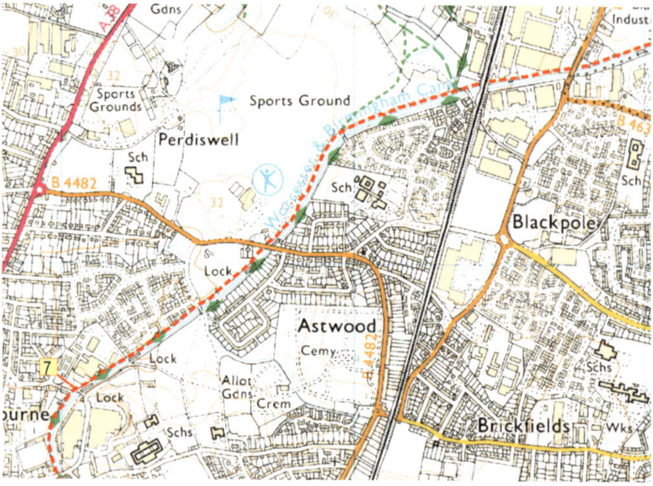

The Severn at Worcester

Leaving this hive of activity behind, we follow the river round to the right (S), **Worcester Cathedral** towering behind an ancient wall. At the first opportunity we turn left (E) away from the river (Wp.3 9M), lines on the wall indicating high water marks of past floods. After passing through ornate gates we ascend steps into the cathedral close; so quiet considering its proximity to the city centre.

A little to the left, we go beside the cathedral to pass under the archway of **Edgar Tower** then along **Edgar Street** with its attractive Georgian houses back into the hubbub of traffic.

Cathedral Close

Turning right (SE), we cross a dual carriageway at traffic lights and follow signs towards the **Commandery Museum**, its wall display of pikes and helmets to our left a reminder of the Battle of Worcester, last of the civil war.

Looking down, it's clear that the wall is part of a bridge over a canal; immediately after it we turn left (Wp.4 16M). It may not seem there's a way through, but at the end of black railings there's a gap before the building in front of us. We pass through it onto the towpath at **Sidbury Lock**, then turn right to head along the canal.

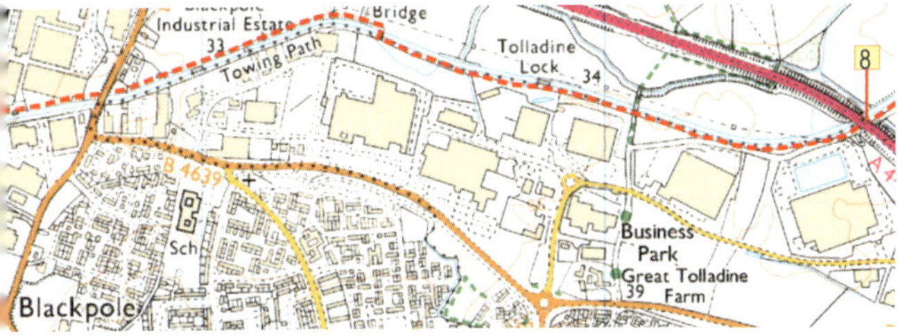

Worcester and Birmingham Canal

Our way, initially on scrunchy gravel has an air of being within the city but not part of it; perhaps it's the quietness and slow speed of travel on the water rather than the roar and rush of cars above that creates this impression.

At the next lock, black bricks neatly protrude from neighbouring red ones to ensure a non-slip surface as we make a rare change of altitude. After the towpath surface changes to tarmac the canal swings left (N) and we go up steps to our right (Wp.5 24M) just before a bridge, then cross it to continue on the left-hand side of the canal.

Our way passes under numerous bridges, beside industrial buildings and a large retirement home, before joining a road for a short distance as it crosses a bridge over a branch of the canal leading to a canal basin. After passing under a high railway viaduct (Wp.6 30M), we're back on the towpath, passing the backs of terraced houses on the left and well-tended allotments beyond bulrushes on the right, then a splendid cricket pitch, **The Cavalier** pub and towering lights behind corrugated iron fencing indicating a football stadium. The canal swings right (NE) to reach bridge 13 (Wp.7 45M) where we must cross back to the right-hand side again.

We pass several locks where narrow boats negotiate the changes of water level. At crumbling bridge 16 the going changes back to gravel, while beyond bridge 19 there's a popular fishing area. Immediately after going under a main-ish road, the Worcester City Boundary is marked by a curious stone surrounded by wooden benches (Wp.8 92M).

This is how it's done!

After a black metal footbridge crosses the canal we come to a staircase of locks and begin to count them as the sound of a motorway rumbles to our right. Just before the fifth, we follow a 'cycle path 45' sign right (Wp.9 104M) into a lane running beside the canal, then go left at a T junction over a bridge (N).

Leaving the canal, we go up a lane first past business units, ignoring footpath signs to left and right. After passing between high hedges and **Offerton Cottages** we reach a T junction (Wp.10 116M). Our way is left towards **Martin Hussingtree**, then immediately right through a gate by a hand-painted black on yellow 'Woodlands' sign, proceeding down the right hand side of a field on grass again.

At the field corner (Wp.11 121M) a metal gate with a helpful way-pointer takes us through into another field to follow its left-hand side which winds its way towards what looks like a wood. But beside the 'wood' we locate a stile hidden in a hedge (Wp.12 126M) and realise that it's only a row of mature trees bounding the field. Now we're in a world of very long grass and tall cow parsley, following a beaten path through it to reach a metal gate (Wp.13 130M). First we follow the left-hand edge of the field before us, then where the edge swings left, we cut across the field towards the right of a hay barn. Here (Wp.14 138M), a track takes us to a lane (Wp.15 140M) to turn left (W) past houses until it turns left itself (Wp.16 142M).

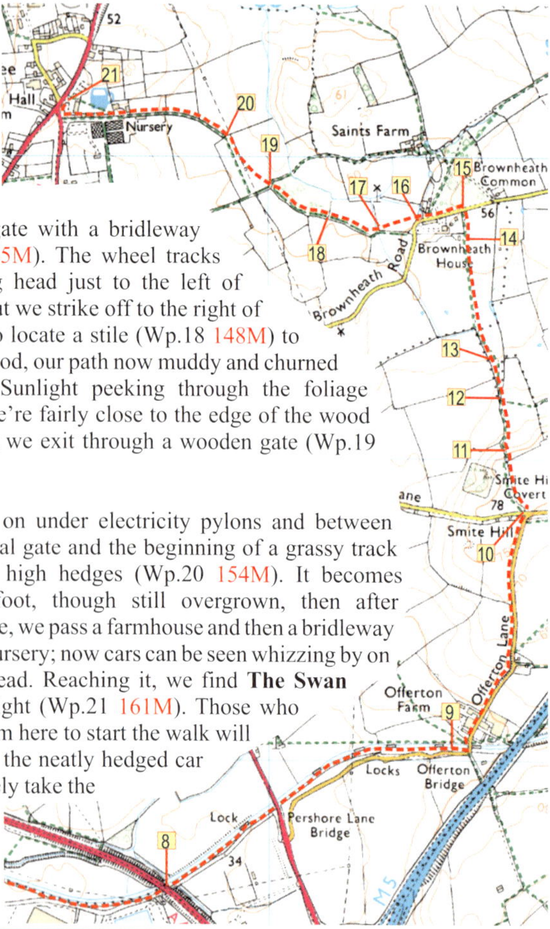

Straight on takes us through a metal gate onto a track and through a field that slowly swings left to another metal gate with a bridleway sign (Wp.17 145M). The wheel tracks we're following head just to the left of woods ahead, but we strike off to the right of them (WNW) to locate a stile (Wp.18 148M) to head into the wood, our path now muddy and churned up by horses. Sunlight peeking through the foliage indicates that we're fairly close to the edge of the wood and before long we exit through a wooden gate (Wp.19 151M).

We go straight on under electricity pylons and between thistles to a metal gate and the beginning of a grassy track hemmed in by high hedges (Wp.20 154M). It becomes gravelly underfoot, though still overgrown, then after another little gate, we pass a farmhouse and then a bridleway to the left by a nursery; now cars can be seen whizzing by on a main road ahead. Reaching it, we find **The Swan** around to the right (Wp.21 161M). Those who took the bus from here to start the walk will find their car in the neatly hedged car park; alternatively take the N° 144 or 244 back to the city centre.

12 HANLEY CASTLE & HANLEY SWAN

We link contrasting pubs - **The Three Kings** in **Hanley Castle**, an old-fashioned, one-roomed real-ale tavern and **The Swan** in **Hanley Swan**, a large modernised hostelry with sofas, a fine restaurant and en-suite rooms with this route through **Merevale Woods**, along a green lane and around **Blackmore End** returning after lunch through **Gilberts End** and the site which gives **Hanley Castle** its name.

Access by car:
From junction 1 of the M50 head towards **Worcester** on the A38, turn left onto the A4104 to **Upton upon Severn** then after a bridge over the **River Severn**, go right onto the B4211. Reaching a village sign for 'Hanley Castle', turn left into a lane signposted 'Hanley Castle High School'. After passing the school, park in front of **The Three Kings** behind a green. OS Grid reference : SO 83873 42010 Nearest postcode : WR8 0BL.

Access by bus:
Bus Nº363 runs hourly from **Great Malvern** to **Hanley Castle** (not Sun).

The Three Kings

Facing **The Three Kings** (Wp.1 0M) we head off to the right down a track (NW) between hedges to a kissing gate and a classic English village cricket ground. Following its left hand perimeter, we pass through a rusty kissing gate (Wp.2 2M) into a bounded gravel path with views left across to the **Malvern Hills**

After passing a pond to our right and a line of caravans to our left, we reach another kissing gate (Wp.3 6M), cross a lane and find another kissing gate a little to the left. Going diagonally across a field of cows (NNW), we pass through yet another kissing gate (Wp.4 10M) to cross a larger road. Over a stile on the other side of the road, we follow the left-hand side of a field by woodland (N) to reach a further stile close to a water trough (Wp.5 14M). Following the direction of a waymark arrow, we go half-right (NE) steeply up a hill with no discernible path, to the right of a wood; half-way up it's reassuring to find a stile (Wp.6 16M).

We plunge into this enchanting wood (NNW), now on a clearly defined path where some of the trees appear to be festooned with spiders' webs. By a waypoint post the path suddenly turns right (NE) and climbs a bit before meeting a green lane (Wp.7 25M) where we go left (NNW) and steadily down. Leaving the woods, we walk between cow parsley with buttercups; after swinging to the left (NW), we pass through a metal barred gate (Wp.8 33M) into a field of friendly cows. Proceeding up the left-hand side, we come to a similar gate taking us back into the green lane, the **Worcestershire Beacon** now straight ahead.

Where a footpath crosses us (Wp.9 42M) our way becomes a farm track, then a tarmac lane again at a farmhouse (Wp.10 45M). Shortly after a further farmhouse at a T junction (Wp.11 51M) we go sharp right (NE), seemingly back on ourselves but then we spot a footpath sign hidden in a hedge (Wp.12 54M), cross a bridge and a stile and go up the left hand side of a field of sheep (N).

.. a path blitzed through..

Veering a little to the right, we cross a ditch before aiming for and crossing a stile in the left hand corner (Wp.13 59M), then it's right (ENE) on a lane past **Blackmore End Cottage** and left (NW) over a stile immediately beyond it. A modern kissing gate leads to a weed-killer blitzed path through a cereal crop, then a bridge and stile (Wp.14 66M). We take the right option over another bridge and along the left-hand edge of a field (W) where the rest of the field is fenced and topped with barbed wire.

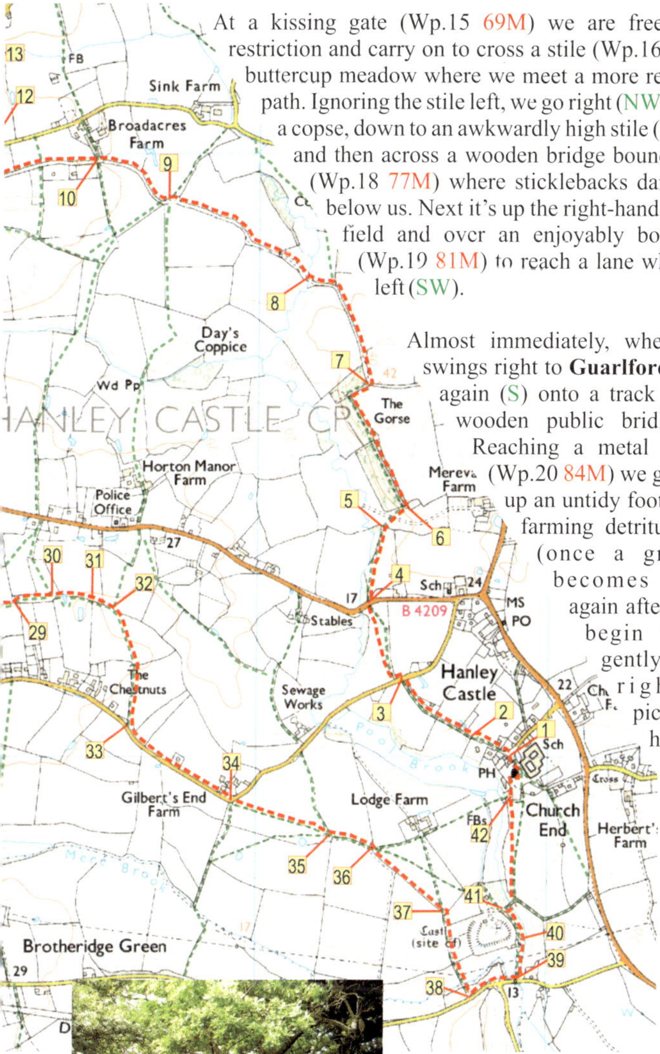

At a kissing gate (Wp.15 69M) we are freed from this restriction and carry on to cross a stile (Wp.16 72M) into a buttercup meadow where we meet a more regularly used path. Ignoring the stile left, we go right (NW), initially by a copse, down to an awkwardly high stile (Wp.17 75M) and then across a wooden bridge bounded by stiles (Wp.18 77M) where sticklebacks dart to and fro below us. Next it's up the right-hand side of a pea field and over an enjoyably bouncy bridge (Wp.19 81M) to reach a lane where we turn left (SW).

Almost immediately, where the lane swings right to **Guarlford**, we go left again (S) onto a track following a wooden public bridleway sign. Reaching a metal barred gate (Wp.20 84M) we go to its right up an untidy footpath around farming detritus, our path (once a green lane) becomes charming again after a gate. We begin to ascend gently, swinging right (SW), picturing cows heading to market along here.

.. picture cows heading to market ..

A footpath crosses us and we turn left (SSE) over a bridge and stile (Wp.21 95M), then cross a path of wood chippings before reaching another stile.

Keeping to the left of the field, we drop steeply to a track over a bridge (Wp.22 99M) then back into a field to go up the other side and over a stile to the right of a metal barred gate (Wp.23 103M) and a lane; it takes us (SE) between well-maintained wooden fences past **Home Farm Stables**.

After the surface changes beside a pleasant avenue of oaks, we reach a magnificent village duck pond and, across a road, our lunch stop, **The Swan** (Wp.24 121M).

The Swan

Refreshed, we make our way across the village green under a spreading oak tree, cross the main B4209 and take the **Welland** road left of the village stores (SSW).

At a signpost to 'Picken End' (Wp.25 126M) we turn left (E) down a residential road, going through a kissing gate at its end (Wp.26 131M) to continue in the same direction, down the right-hand side of a meadow. There are confusing waypoint arrows half left and half right at the next stile (Wp.27 135M) but we make for the stile visible pretty much straight ahead (Wp.28 137M). This time we follow the waypoint direction along the left-hand side of a field. At a further stile by a water trough (Wp29 139M) we head into scrubby woodland until we come to a meeting of ways (Wp.30 141M).

The footpath straight on is not a right of way so we turn right over a bridge adjoining a couple of stiles, ignoring a path to the right, to leave this wooded area at a further stile (Wp.31 143M). Where there are options to left and right (Wp.32 145M) we go right (S) between fences restraining horses, onto a track and through a gate to meet a lane (Wp.33 151M). Here we turn left (SE) and carry on until it swings left at **Gilbert Ends Farm** (Wp.34 157M) where our way is straight on through another blitzed field (ESE).

At its far side we join another path (Wp.35 163M) and keep along the left-hand side of the next field with the spire of a church in **Upton upon Severn** dead ahead. A rusty kissing gate (Wp.36 167M) takes us a little to the left and we continue along the right-hand side of the next field (SE) to the far corner (Wp.37 174M) where we find a track (S). After two gates and a plethora of toll ride signs, a metal gate heralds a lane (Wp.38 179M) where we turn left (ENE) then immediately after a lane to the right, we follow a footpath sign (Wp.39 181M) left up the drive of a house (N).

Past the house, we find a stile to the left of a metal gate (Wp.40 183M) into woodland, blackberry bushes and walnut trees. Then in quick succession and generally in the same direction, we go right across water at a stile (Wp.41 185M), straight on at a further stile and left at a kissing gate up the left hand side of a field of potatoes. Leaving the field at a way-point post (Wp.42 190M) we ignore a path descending steeply left, before a kissing gate takes us into a churchyard. Circling around to the right of the church, we pass a war memorial and go through a rickety gate to find ourselves back at **The Three Kings** (Wp.1 194M).

13 MADRESFIELD COURT

The maximum height of 55 metres above sea level attained during this walk is a clear indication that it's pretty much on the flat! From **Old Hills**, it goes down to and then beside the **River Severn** through the quiet hamlets of **Pixham** and **Clevelode** before traversing field paths towards the **Malvern Hills** and circling the privately owned **Madresfield Court** with its perfectly maintained estate.

Access by car:
From junction 7 of the M5, head towards **Worcester**. At the first roundabout turn left and follow signs for the A449 to 'Malvern'. In **Powick** turn left onto the B4424, pass through **Callow End** and where the road swings right and then left, park in the **Old Hills** car park on the right. OS Grid reference: SO 82951 48723 Nearest postcode: WR2 4TQ.

Access by bus:
Bus Nº 363 runs hourly from **Great Malvern** to **Old Hills** (not Sun).

From the car park (Wp.1 0M) we cross the road and walk back along the grass verge (NE) to **Pixham Ferry Lane** (a quiet lane signposted 'Pixham', Wp.2 3M). The lane's name recalls the time when it led to a passenger ferry across the river; we follow it (E) through woodland. At one point well-constructed new wooden steps climb the bank, access for a mobile phone mast. After a gentle descent with trees meeting overhead, we attain the flood plain of **Severn Plain** and continue past a 'No Through Road' sign to an Elizabethan manor house; the lane swings right (SE) and we reach a picnic site by the river (Wp.3 18M) with a tiny stone landing stage.

Retracing our steps (NW) past **Pixham Manor House** and back to the 'No Through Road' sign (Wp.4 22M), we ignore the lane right to 'Callow End' and go left (SSW) across a cattle grid and along a flat tarmac track between fields. Ahead and right is **Pixham Farm** but we fork left (Wp.5 25M S) away from the track leading to the farm, onto a grassy path beside a hedge. After a metal barred gate the way continues as a flinty track along the left side of a field by a hedge, **Bredon Hill** visible in the distance away to our left. After another metal barred gate our way goes diagonally right (SW) to the left of a pylon and a sluice gate then around to the right through an open metal gate (Wp.6 36M) to another metal barred gate and bridge over **Madresfield Brook**. After the bridge we follow the left hand field edge (SSW) beside a copse (with a pervading scent of bluebells in spring), then go diagonally right following the footpath through a field (W) to meet a track (Wp.7 46M) which takes us (SW) past attractive barn conversions and **Clevelode Farm House**, reaching a lane (Wp.8 49M).

Turning left (SE) down the lane, we make a brief detour through **Clevelode**, reaching a grassy area by the river with a wooden landing stage, a great place for a picnic (Wp.9 52M). Both the hamlets of **Pixham** and **Clevelode** are well off the tourist beat and feel untouched by time which makes them even more attractive. Returning up the lane (NW) to Wp.8, we continue swinging left

(SW) with footpaths to left and right and pass a toll house to reach and cross the main road (Wp.10 63M). We turn right (NW) to walk along the wide grass verge, passing a footpath on the left before reaching a tarmac lane (Wp.11 67M). A few metres down it we approach the imposing entrance to **Whiteacres Farm** looking for a waypost pointing to a stile which leads us to a nondescript path (WNW) running between it and the adjoining property. At the rear of the two properties (Wp.12 72M) we go over a stile and along the left edge of a small duck and chicken filled field owned by the adjoining property, then over another stile into a 'proper' farmer's field.

.. great views along the Malvern Hills ..

We follow the field's right hand edge, swinging left (WSW) with great views along the **Malvern Hills**, then right (NW), climbing gently.

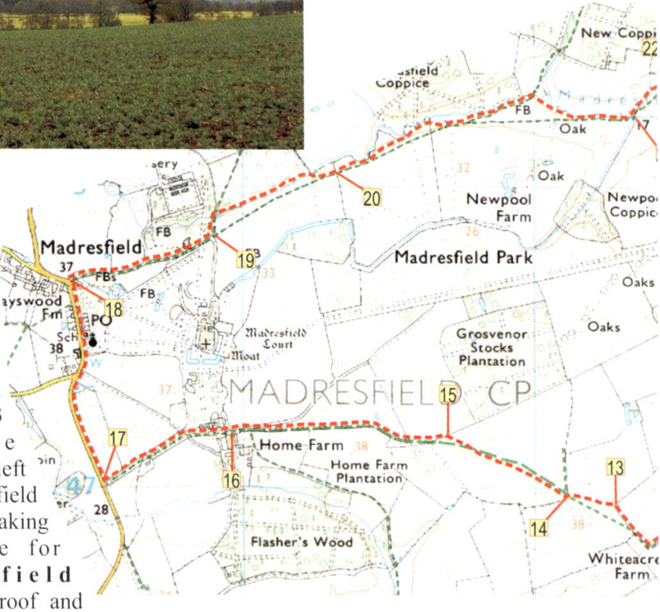

However, where it swings right again (Wp.13 77M) we strike out left across the field (WNW), making a bee-line for **Madresfield Court**, its roof and chimneys just visible.

Madresfield Court

We find a gate hidden in the hedge (Wp.14 81M) leading to a path cleared thorugh a cereal crop to access the next field. At the other side (Wp.15 87M) we veer left along a track (W) following blue bridleway signs then dink right-left to go through a metal barred gate with **Malvern** straight ahead and

Madresfield Court now to our right.

The track leads through **Home Farm** (Wp.16 98M) with an unusual French-style dovecote on the left, where it morphs into a well-made tarmac track running between lime trees to cross a cattle grid by an Elizabethan lodge to meet a road (Wp.17 105M). We turn right (NNW) and may see a Morgan from the factory on test; **Malvern** is not only the home of Morgans but the Santler Car which was reputedly the first four-wheel, petrol driven vehicle made in Britain, tested around **Madresfield Court** as the speed limit on public highways was then 4mph!

The French-style dovecote, Home Farm (Wp.16)

Passing the 'Madresfield' village sign, we come upon an imposing church on the right and a red ivy-encrusted telephone box on the left before remarking on the estate houses, reminiscent of a bygone era.

Where the road swings left (Wp.18 114M) we go right (E) between gateposts by a prominent tree surrounded by white stones, along a tarmac track signposted 'Three Choirs Way', a long distance footpath linking the cathedrals of **Worcester**, **Hereford** and **Gloucester**.

At a fork we go right with conifers to our left and an orchard to our right as we skirt **Madresfield Court** then drop down to go under two brick-built arched bridges. Beyond these, where the track swings right, we go left to a metal kissing gate beside a wooden barred gate (Wp.19 121M) and on the other side of it, left again (N) along a field edge. Our way leads us to a metal barred gate but instead of following the obvious way through it we head right (ENE) in front of it along the left field edge with a strip of scrubby woodland separating us from the next field. Ignoring first a stile and then a metal barred gate to the left, we continue in the same direction to reach a waymarked stile to the right of a metal barred gate (Wp.20 129M).

.. a waypost confirms our route ..

Our route goes beside **Woodsfield Coppice**, twice cutting corners by going between a cereal crop where the alternative would have been particularly circuitous.

A waypost confirms our route; we ignore a path that crosses us before coming to a footbridge (Wp.21 144M) taking us back across **Madresfield Brook** into an enormous field of sheep and horses. The temptation is to continue along the brook but we follow the direction of the waymark arrow, diagonally right (NE) up the field to another waypost at the corner of **New Coppice** (Wp.22 147M).

We cross a track to run along the top of the field and in the corner find a wooden kissing gate to the right of a padlocked metal gate (Wp.23 152M). On the other side, over a track, we're presented with the only climb of the walk - shame it's right at the end (if it's too daunting an alternative is right along the track to meet the road where turning left returns us to the car). The grassy footpath takes us steeply up between 'No Horses' signs and vibrant gorse to a bench at the top (Wp.24 156M); there's a trig point to our left, the car park down to our right and **Worcester** in the far distance. Steadily down (E) to the car park (Wp.1 159M), a chicken wire-covered plank bridge brings us safely back to our start.

14 THE FULL MONTY

Our walk follows the top of the ridge along the **Malvern Hills** including 15 named summits. After some discussion over which direction to walk as both had their merits, we agreed to do it south to north as, that way, there was a pub close to the finish! Unfortunately, there's no public transport, though a taxi from **North Quarry Car Park** back to the start is a viable option. Much of the way is easy to follow and parts of the route are covered in Walks 16, 17, 18, 19, 22 and 23 in this book, therefore we've not repeated so much detail in this walk description though it's comprehensive enough for you to find your way.

Access by car:
From Junction 2 of the M50, head towards **Ledbury** on the A417 then take the first road on the right to **Bromsberrow**. In the village go right and left towards **Whiteleaved Oak** and park on the right in a small lay-by under an oak tree. A **Chase End Hill** information board confirms you're in the right place. OS Grid reference: SO 75721 34895 Nearest postcode: HR8 1SE.

From the information board (Wp.1 0M) we set off steadily up the obvious path (NE) through woodland. After a smaller path forks left, we find ourselves on a wide grassy path between bracken. Another large path joins us from the right, then at a fork either choice will take us to our first summit of **Chase End Hill** (Wp.2 11M); that didn't take long!

Next it's very steeply down to the left (NNW) until we are engulfed in shrubbery, where the descent lessens. After a wooden gate we're in a sunken lane that emerges by a cottage to a lane (Wp.3 19M). Right (NE) takes us through tranquil **Whiteleaved Oak** where Gloucestershire, Herefordshire and Worcestershire meet; after the lane swings right (E) we go left up a track and through a wooden gate behind a house.

Whiteleaved Oak

Just after the track swings left we take a narrow, stony path even further left (Wp.4 22M) that goes steeply up (NW) which flattens off before leading us right and left, aided by a waymarker nailed to a post. Now it's steeply up again under overhanging trees with dead leaves underfoot until we emerge close to the top of **Ragged Stone Hill**, its summit only a few rocky steps further on (Wp.5 33M). Keeping straight along the ridge with the obelisk dead ahead (see Walk 21 Eastnor Park), we begin descending, taking the rightmost steeper, faster option that takes us down through bracken with foxgloves dotted here and there.This time we don't reach trees until we're close to the main road, reached via a kissing gate. We go right along the pavement (ENE) and across the road to a car park (Wp.6 44M); to the right of a track with a cattle grid, a metal gate leads to our path going steeply up a field (N).

Again there are two choices; we take the left to continue steeply up through woodland - maybe the hardest climb of the walk - and we pass a National Trust sign engulfed in bracken before reaching the summit of **Midsummer Hill** (Wp.7 58M). Its ugly shelter and information board may be useful though from an aesthetic point of view, they mar this special place.

The Obelisk from Midsummer Hill

We start our descent by continuing along the ridge but swing left (W), down to meet a gravel track (Wp.8 64M). Right (NNW) takes us further down through a gate with a waymark to a cattle grid (Wp.9 69M). Straight on would take us to the obelisk but before crossing the cattle grid we go right (N) through a new metal gate, into woodland on a rutted track which swings further right (NE). Approaching a second cattle grid we take a path a little to the right and go through a wooden gate (Wp.10 78M) then right again onto a broad path and steadily uphill (E) passing a small toposcope before a few steps take us up to the ridge then left (N) to **Swinyard Hill** (Wp.11 83M).

Following the obvious way along the ridge, we descend gently to meet a lower path (Wp.12 91M) but soon take a right (E) helpfully signposted 'Hangman's Hill' and it's steeply up again, swinging back to the left (N) to attain this summit (Wp.13 98M). As we progress further north and closer to **Great Malvern** the paths are more regularly used; we meet many more walkers so there's no mistaking our next objective, **Millennium Hill**, over to the left. First, though, it's down to a larger toposcope (NW) then up a well-maintained set of zigzagging steps, our climb lessening before we reach the top (Wp.14 104M).

Another down and up takes us to **Herefordshire Beacon** (Wp.15 110M), probably the most visited summit - though not the highest, it offers spectacular views in all directions. A tarmac way leads us down (NE); we spot cars through the trees beforc reaching a large car park via a wooden gate and cross a main road to the **Malvern Hills Hotel**, a good lunch stop (Wp.16 122M).

Our way down from Herefordshire Beacon

On leaving the hotel, we go around to the right to follow a minor road (NNE and toilets on the left) and take a path on the right (not the steepest one) up between rosebay willow herb into a well-laid out **Malvern Hills Conservators Car Park**. From its far corner the series of summits we have yet to conquer rise ahead. We begin a gentle ascent on the metalled path (NE) towards them; the view to the left begins to open up, then at a fork (Wp.17 132M) leave the path and strike out to the right (NNE) now climbing more steeply to reach the top of **Black Hill** (Wp.18 138M). Once again we enjoy magnificent 360° views before heading down and up (N) on our self-propelled roller coaster ride to our next summit of **Pinnacle Hill**, fooled, not for the first time today, by its false summit (Wp.19 148M).

A similar pattern leads us to our next summit of **Jubilee Hill** (Wp.20 152M) but this time it's not so far down before we ascend again, a delightful example of ridge walking as we travel between two worlds below and somehow separate from us. At the base of **Jubilee Hill** a grove of conifers offers welcome shade on hot days. There's another smaller bump (Wp.21 159M) before we reach **Perseverance Hill** (Wp.22 167M), distinguished by its plateau summit. We keep left of the ridge as we descend to **Wyche Cutting**, coming down almost on top of a bus stop (Wp.23 172M) behind

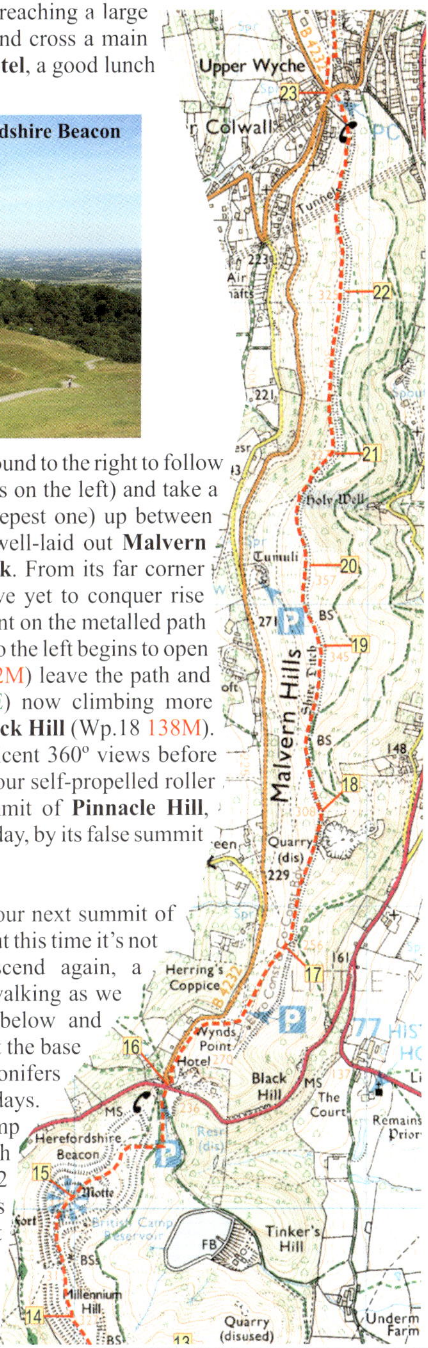

which are further toilets. **The Wyche Inn** is along the road to the right; however, we press on across the road and up **Beacon Road** to the right, passing a car park on the left with a useful information board describing the whole length of the hills as we keep to the right up the main tarmac way, steadily ascending. After passing a further car park, and another toposcope and black post restricting vehicles (Wp.24 178M), we strike off to the right through gorse bushes, our way clearly visible ahead, going in the same direction as the tarmac but just a soupçon apart, comfortable reaching **Summer Hill**'s summit (Wp.25 191M).

Continuing in the same direction, we make for the highest point of the range, again with a false summit that's followed by a gentle ascent. This time there's a trig point and a substantial toposcope - we're at **Worcestershire Beacon** (Wp.26 199M). Now it's down, down, down to the head of **Happy Valley** where a plethora of paths meet up at another circular set of directions. **North Hill**, straight ahead, is our next objective. Our way is up to its left. A larger path joins us from the left (Wp.27 216M) before we take a right turn (E) and scramble to the top (Wp.28 223M) - phenomenal!

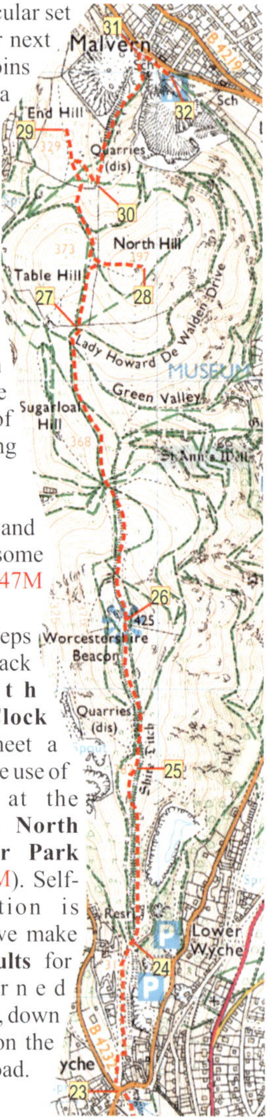

We retrace our steps and turn right (N) then fork left (NNW) to add the smaller but psychologically significant **End Hill** (Wp.29 232M) to our tally of summits. Again we retrace our steps down but this time before starting to climb again, we go left (SE) down to a lightning-struck tree (Wp.30 236M), then left again (NNE). Now we're clearly coming down off the range and it's steep all the way, the buildings of **North Malvern**, initially far below us, becoming clearer.

Steps, awkward for tired legs, help us zigzag left and right. Just after a black railing aids us down some particularly steep steps, we turn right (Wp.31 247M ESE) by an ivy-clad wall.

North Malvern Clock Tower

After more steps we pass the back of **North Malvern Clock Tower** to meet a road and make use of the bench at the entrance to **North Quarry Car Park** (Wp.32 251M). Self-congratulation is justified as we make for **The Vaults** for well-earned refreshments, down to the right on the Worcester Road.

15 BETWEEN GREAT MALVERN & COLWALL STATIONS

From **Great Malvern Station** to next stop on the line **Colwall Station**, we cross **Malvern Common**, passing **Worcestershire Golf Club** before climbing over the top of **The Malverns** to **The Kettle Sings** and down through fields to **Colwall**. It takes only five minutes by train yet our two hour walk is amply rewarded. If you fancy a coffee before setting off, the **Lady Foley Tea Rooms** at **Great Malvern Station** are a cut above the average station offering and was once Lady Foley's personal waiting room!

Great Malvern Station

Access by train:
Great Malvern has good connections with London Paddington and Birmingham New Street (details:- 08457 484950 or www.nationalrail.co.uk).

Access by car:
From junction 7 of the M5 head towards **Worcester**. At the first roundabout turn left and follow signs for the A449 and 'Malvern'. After passing though **Malvern Link** we turn left at traffic lights signposted 'Town Centre'. At the second set of lights in the centre of **Great Malvern**, turn left again then fork right; the station is on the right. OS Grid reference: SO 78292 45688 Nearest postcode: WR14 3AU.

We leave the station (Wp.1 0M) and go left on its approach road (W). At a T junction we turn left (SSW) into a leafy residential road with our first glimpse of the **Malvern Hills** up to our right. At a further T junction we turn left again (SE) by a spreading chestnut tree, then go under a railway bridge and past **The Morgan** to reach a T junction with a larger road (Wp.2 5M), going right (SW) opposite a baker's and by a classic black and white timbered cottage. We take the first right (Wp.3 8M NW), an acute turn into **Woodshears Road** and pass back under the railway to find a footpath immediately on our left (Wp.4 10M).

We're heading between fences (SSW) in an area filled with cow parsley, the railway embankment up to our left. Over another road and through a black kissing gate to **Malvern Common**, we keep left alongside the railway and climb gently until we're above it. Nordic conifers seem out of place in this otherwise quintessentially English environment of mown grass and mature deciduous trees.

Dropping down while keeping close by the railway, we look for an easily-missed tiny tunnel beneath it (Wp.5 23M). Through it, we swing right then fork left (SSE), still across grass, to reach and cross **Peachfield Road** (Wp.6 27M) enjoying great views of **Bredon Hill** left, the houses of **Wyche Cutting** breaking up the otherwise continuous green of the **Malvern Hills** to our right. We follow a tarmac track (SW) diagonally right and are soon presented with a row of houses. We go to the right of all but one of them to find a wooden gate (Wp.7 29M SE), swinging sharp right at the back of the houses around the garden of the last of them. With a golf course on our left, it's then more gently back left (SW) to continue on a well-defined path with a mad jumble of luxuriant growth on both sides. Emerging from what's now woodland, we swing slightly left (SSW) and cross the golf course to more woods where the path becomes a track. After ignoring a path left by a stream and a bridleway right, we pop out into the open again with the prestigious **Worcestershire Golf Course** clubhouse ahead.

.. to a new metal barred gate ..

On reaching its car park we turn right (W), make for an arch in a tall hedge (Wp.8 42M) and continue in the same direction between trees with no obvious path to a new metal barred gate. Now we begin steadily ascending across a field and swinging slightly right, (WNW) unfortunately between fences; it's quite a pull so it's worth stopping for a breather and a look back to **Bredon Hill** when we reach another metal gate.

Our ascent continues up a concrete track to cross a main road (Wp.9 53M) and find our continuation on a well-made tarmac path between stone walls which rises above the road. We go left across a minor road and further up a very steep path between houses with an essential handrail. At the top it's left along a road (S), thankfully now on the flat, and past a 'No Through Road' sign with houses to the right, the land to our left dropping away steeply revealing fantastic views. Later the situation reverses as beech woodland clings to the steep slope to the right as we pass houses to the left.

Over a wall between them we look down to the golf clubhouse - it's amazing how high we've just climbed. At the end of the road (Wp.10 59M) we follow a wooden 'Public Bridleway' sign up a tarmac and mud track (S). Passing to the right of a house, a well-trodden path takes us steadily up through woodland past the remnants of quarrying to our right, with views across the **Severn** valley to our left.

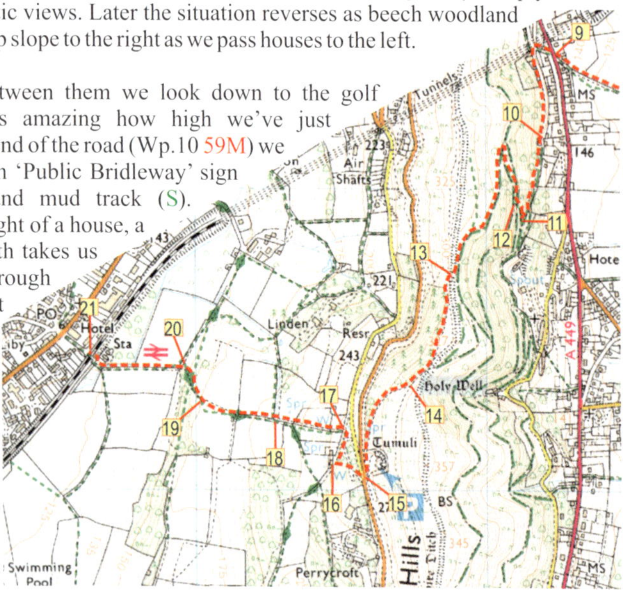

We keep right at a fork, then (Wp.11 64M) turn sharp right (NW), the first of many sharp turns as our path zigzags up this side of the hill, easing the gradient. We meet a path folowing the contour (Wp.12 66M), a concrete sign to 'Holywell' embedded in a brick surround to our left and a bench to the right.

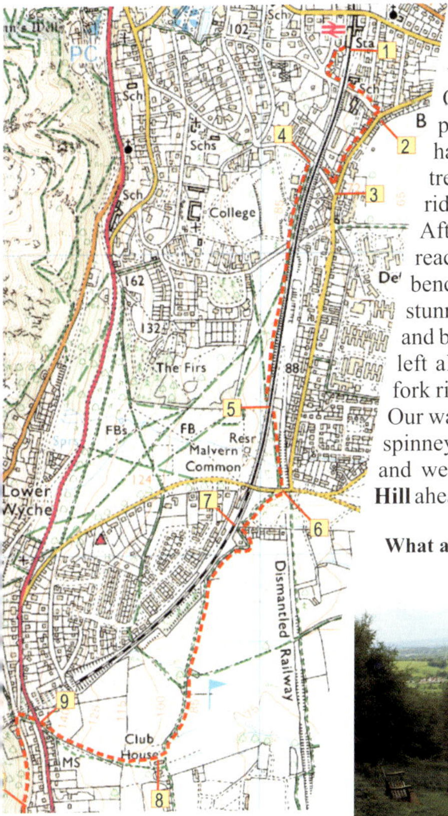

Our way is across it and left (ESE) then almost immediately right (N), the steepest of the alternatives. Continuing steadily up, we ignore a path to our right before reaching a hairpin left. Leaving the shelter of the trees, we swing to the right (SW), the ridge visible above us and to the right. After crossing a larger path just before reaching the ridge, a perfectly sited bench (Wp.13 77M) invites us to take in stunning views both ahead to the west and behind to the east. Continuing, we go left along the well-trodden path (S) and fork right around the base of **Jubilee Hill**. Our way is still gently upward, now with a spinney to our right, but soon flattens off and we see the next summit of **Pinnacle Hill** ahead.

What a position! (bench after Wp.14)

Forking right and almost immediately right again (Wp.14 82M SW), we begin descending steadily with the village of **Colwall** to our right while the railway tunnels beneath us as it snakes its way to **Ledbury** and on to **Hereford**. The ideal positioning of a bench to the left of the path can make it a challenge to find space on it. Descending further and swinging left (SSW), **British Camp** is visible through the trees.

After passing two more benches we arrive at **Gardiner's Quarry**, now a car park, with its useful information board (Wp.15 89M). On the other side of a road we spot the sign for 'The Kettle Sings' and make straight for the single storey building below. (WNW). Recommended for lunch or a snack, it has great views westward, particularly from the outside seating area reached by steps down to the right of the building (Wp.16 91M).

Turning left after the few steps up from the entrance (NNE), our way is along a tarmac track. Where it swings right, back up to the road, we continue straight ahead on a grassy track to find a public footpath sign down to the left (Wp.17 93M) which leads us over a rusty metal stile (W) beside a wooden gate. Soon **Colwall** is spread out below us. To the left of a gate we drop steeply between fences, going left at a T junction of paths (Wp.18 98M) through a wooden gate. A duck board helps us to cross a muddy ditch, then we head immediately right to continue in the same direction, a row of beeches to our left and a hedge to our right.

After another wooden gate we continue across a field in the same direction towards trees, with little sign of a path until we spot a waymark post (Wp.19 103M) directing us right (N) along the bottom of the field with a steep drop to our left. then it's down through a wood (NW) to cross the **Worcestershire Way**. Further down some steps, we swing left (W) to a wooden gate (Wp.20 105M) and follow the right hand field edge, an ancient oak at the field's centre. In the corner of the field we ford a stream where ducks quack noisily, go through a kissing gate and much to our surprise - there's **Colwall Station**!

We cross the metal railway bridge to reach the platform (Wp.21 112M), ready for our return, or if refreshments are required first, just along the station approach road **Colwall Park** is happy to offer all the usual facilities of a country hotel - as long as you remove your boots!

16 NORTH HILL FROM LINK COMMON

North Hill, at 398 metres second only to **Worcestershire Beacon** in height, dominates the skyline as we set out to reach its summit in only a smidgen over 45 minutes rewarded with stunning, uncluttered views north and east; then we visit **St Ann's Well Café** on the way back down. But be warned, although the walk is short a good deal of puff is required!

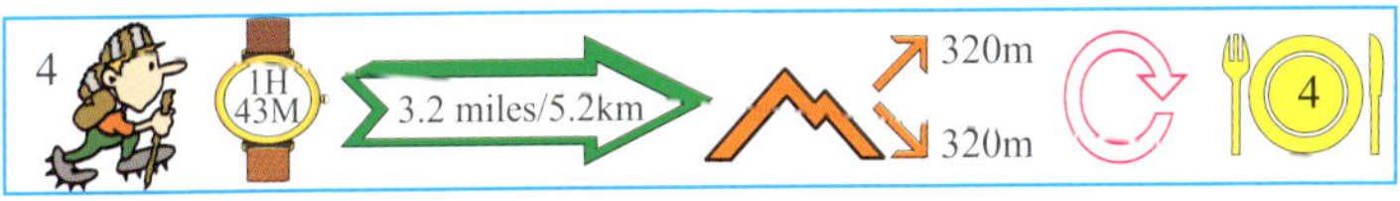

Access by car:
From junction 7 of the M5, head towards **Worcester**, turning left at the first roundabout and following signs for the A449 and **Malvern**. After passing though **Malvern Link**, take the first left after the common appears to the left; the car park is on the right in the dip. OS Grid reference: SO 77888 47051 Nearest postcode: WR14 2TZ.

Access by bus:
Not necessary from **Great Malvern** as the start is only a short jaunt from the town centre.

North Hill from Link Common

From the car park in the middle of **Link Common** (Wp.1 0M), our objective of **North Hill** sits fair and square in front of us. We follow a path ascending gently across the common towards it (WSW), passing several attractive buildings on our left.

At its edge we go over a crossroads (Wp.2 3M) then swing right at first (W) beside the common but soon go left into **Link Terrace** (Wp.3 5M), climbing steadily and aiming to the right of a church steeple which peers down from behind trees. On reaching the back of **The Vaults** pub we go to the right of it, to traffic lights and crossing these, continue steadily ascending in the same direction, passing **Holy Trinity Church** on our right. A bench marks the extent of the common in this direction; we continue up to reach a diagonal cross roads (Wp.4 10M).

Again we go straight across (WNW), now on the larger **North Malvern Road,** ignoring tempting steps up the side of the hill. Just after the entrance to **North Quarry Car Park** (Wp.5 16M) we take a path to the left (SW) for a steady climb to **North Malvern Clock Tower**; then brick reinforced steps take us to join another path on the right. Soon after we take the rightmost of a choice of routes (Wp.6 18M), up more steps contained within a brick surround. We emerge onto a delightful open grass space, once a quarry.

.. higgledy-piggledy steps ..

On the other side, a further set of much more higgledy-piggledy steps take us out of the quarry (S) and steeply up past old workings to reach a larger path (Wp.7 23M). We go right (SSW) and begin serious climbing. The path swings left (E) by a lightning-struck tree (Wp.8 30M); we have a brief respite before climbing steeply again between bracken to reach a track winding its way along the contour (Wp.9 35M).

Now it's right (S), thankfully almost on the flat. After passing a stone sign indicating 'Great Malvern' behind us and 'West Malvern' straight on, we enjoy great views across to the right. The track sweeps to the right (W); the rock indentation on the left would make a fabulous spot to picnic and sunbathe. Then we turn left onto a path by a bench on the right (Wp.10 40M SSW), climbing steeply again

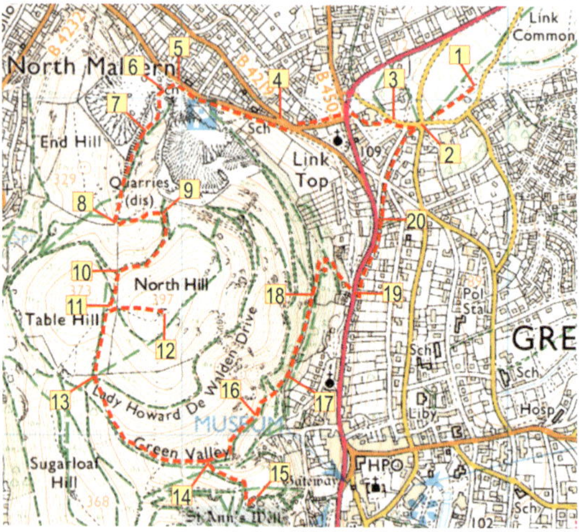

The view from North Hill

Another path joins us from the right before we crest the ridge to see the other side of **Worcestershire Beacon** and beyond (Wp.11 42M) before turning left (E) to climb steeply again between grass to the summit (Wp.12 47M); the views over **Great Malvern** and the **Severn Valley** are just amazing.

Having drunk our fill of the views, we retrace our steps (W) to where we turned to climb the hill (Wp.11 50M), this time turning left (S) with the ridge of the **Malvern Hills** extending away ahead of us. Almost immediately we fork left onto a minor grassy path and descend steadily to reach a track (Wp.13 53M), cross it and go down a couple of steps (SE) onto a wide grassy path between isolated trees.

The density of trees increases as the path swings left (E), a smaller path joins us from the right and a stream pops out from underground to burble beside us.

We meet the original track along which donkeys carried the less able up from **Great Malvern** to **St Ann's Well Café** which hairpins in front of us (Wp.14 61M). We follow it right (ESE) and steadily upwards to another panoramic view with a green circular seat. From here the roof of the café is visible down to our right so we make straight for it (Wp.15 66M).

St. Ann's Well Café

Backtracking to the hairpin (Wp.14 70M), we follow it around to the right then go left, following a sign to 'North Quarry' and 'Ivy Scar Rock'. After a couple of steps up we go right and gently down a wide path (E) through wooded lower slopes. The path narrows and bends left (NE), then at a fork (Wp.16 73M), we go right and steadily down to a meeting of ways. We keep descending in the same direction until we join a larger path (Wp.17 75M) where we go left (NNE) by a wall topped by a fence, following it up and down as if on a roller coaster. As it ends (Wp.18 80M) we take a smaller path on the right to head steadily down and begin to hear traffic noise from the road below. After a tunnel of holly the path begins to drop more steeply, hairpinning right and left before joining a larger path going right (SE) down concrete steps to the main **Worcester Road** (Wp.19 86M).

Turning left (NNE), we pass elegant Georgian houses, almost all converted into flats, and take the second gap in the railings to cross the road and head right down **Bank Street** (Wp.20 89M), between more attractive, albeit smaller, properties. At the bottom, one has a pair of wrought iron horse heads either side of the door - it's the back of the deservedly popular **Nags Head**. Once we reach the crossroads (Wp.2 95M), we're back on our outward path and there's still the common itself to enjoy before returning (NE) to the car park (Wp.1 103M).

17 WORCESTERSHIRE BEACON

A flight of steps off a residential road begins our assault of the **Worcestershire Beacon**. First it's up through woodland to **Wyche Cutting**, then along the ridge to the beacon via **Summer Hill** and down to the café at **St. Ann's Well**, before enjoying a delightful contour path back.

Access by car:
From junction 7 of the M5 head towards **Worcester**. At the first roundabout turn left and follow signs for the A449, first for 'Malvern' then 'Great Malvern'. Continuing on the A449 through **Great Malvern** look out for the village sign for **Malvern Wells** then **The Railway Inn** on the right. Next on the right is **Eaton Road**, a quiet residential road which runs diagonally uphill. Take the first right, **Westminster Road**, sharply back on ourselves and park at the foot of steps up through woodland. OS Grid reference: SO 77160 43508 Nearest postcode: WR14 4PE.

Access by bus:
You could take bus Nº362 or 363, every 30 minutes from **Great Malvern** to the bottom of **Eaton Road** (not Sun).The mile long walk from the town centre, much of it beside the common, is a pleasant alternative.

The flight of steps at the start

We steadily climb the flight of steps (Wp.1 0M) from **Westminster Road** up to **Wyche Cutting** (NW), woodland on both sides. As the way steepens there's a handrail on the right for a short period, then metal railings with houses glimpsed beyond, though woods continue up to the left. Below and right the railway line sweeps round a housing estate before tunnelling beneath us. Near the top a white cottage to our right stands over amazing views while on our left a handrail helps us to the top (Wp.2 8M). We go left into a road for a few steps, steeply upward before swinging around to the right to meet a main road, over which and to the right is **The Wyche Inn**.

Our way is straight across the road and steeply up a tarmac path between houses. After a few steps views open over green railings to **Bredon Hill**, younger cousin to **The Malverns** and visited in Walks 1 to 4. Reaching the top of the short climb we circle around a bungalow named **Ridgeway** (W) with the car park for those driving to the beacon down to our left. At first we drop down as if intending to follow the tarmac, but before reaching it, strike off right onto a smaller path (Wp.3 11M) that swings right then left (N). Ignoring a rocky path up left we enjoy views over **Malvern Common** to **Qinetiq**, a research establishment and mainstay of employment in **Malvern**. Turning

Toposcope at Worcestershire Beacon

right onto the ridge path (Wp.4 15M) we can look back to **British Camp** and forward to **Summer Hill** before dropping down to a concrete, circular waymarker by the tarmac we were seeking to avoid. Undaunted, at the first chance beyond it we swing away right again, climbing steadily between gorse. We

North Hill from Worcestershire Beacon

ignore a path down right (Wp.5 22M) and carry on until we reach open moorland just to the right of the path to the **Summer Hill** summit. The tarmac way has now disappeared around the western side so we move to the left and on towards the summit (Wp.6 27M).

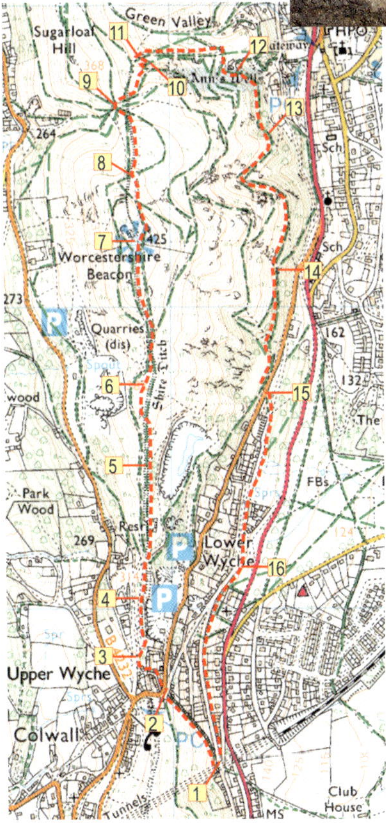

After the summit it's steadily down to a bench with outstanding views including the classic outline of **Malvern St. James School** standing out from surrounding buildings. Crossing the tarmac path, we head up to the next peak, first reaching a false summit with a rocky outcrop to the left but dropping down only slightly before seeing the trig point for **Worcestershire Beacon** ahead (Wp.7 36M). It's worth examining the excellent toposcope close by before clambering down rocks to the right of the direction of the ridge (NE) and crossing a wide path.

Our next objective is an obvious meeting of ways with another concrete, circular waymarker below us and a plethora of paths to it, we select the rightmost grassy one (N) and descend steadily, crossing a larger path (Wp.8 41M) before reaching it (Wp.9 44M). Ahead is **North Hill** with paths straight up it and round both sides as well as paths further to the left and right. Ours is the grassy one further to the right which heads for **Great Malvern** (ENE). This delightful section descends steadily and soon swings left (NE) between gorse and silver birch saplings. It narrows and becomes a bit tricky underfoot, quite a welcome diversion, before we meet another path and turn left (Wp.10 48M NW).

After a steep downhill section we meet a track (Wp.11 49M) and turn right (E), continuing our steady descent until we meet another track and spot the octagonal roof of **St. Ann's Well Café** down to our right (Wp.12 58M).

St. Ann's Well Café

Open every day of the week between Easter and October (Fri/Sat/Sun only in winter), the café is thoroughly recommended for hearty, nutritious food - just the ticket for a day out in the hills!

Facing **St. Ann's Well** we go left on a wide path (SE) along the contour, assisted by a metal handrail at its start. The overall direction is broadly south as it meanders along making easy, relaxed walking through woodland dominated by beech and holly. It's easy to imagine meeting a couple of Victorian ladies in long flowing dresses and parasols along here. We ignore a path down to our left (Wp.13 62M) and another descending steeply before beginning to hear the sound of cars on the road below. A path crosses us diagonally (Wp.14 71M) before we start dropping gently to meet the road going to **Wyche Cutting** (Wp.15 76M).

Crossing, we take a few steps up the hill before turning left down a residential road with open views over the **Severn Valley**, then right (SSW) to continue on the flat parallel to a main road below us. To our right, tiers of houses command a stunning position, then with the local primary school in front of us (Wp.16 85M) we turn right (SW) into **Old Wyche Road** and climb steadily, then take the first left into **Westminster Road** which swings left (S). We pass firstly through woods and then between houses before returning to our car on the right (Wp.1 92M).

18 HOLYWELL & 'THE KETTLE SINGS'

What a lovely little walk! Only three and a half miles with no steep ascents or descents yet offering the contrasting views of the flat **Severn Plain** in the east and over the wooded ridges of Herefordshire to the **Black Mountains** in the west. Starting part way up the eastern side from **Malvern Wells** enables us to reach the ridge in twenty minutes and then it's down the other side to a really scrummy tearoom (closed Mondays except for July and August) and back over the top further south, this time taking in **Holywell Spring**.

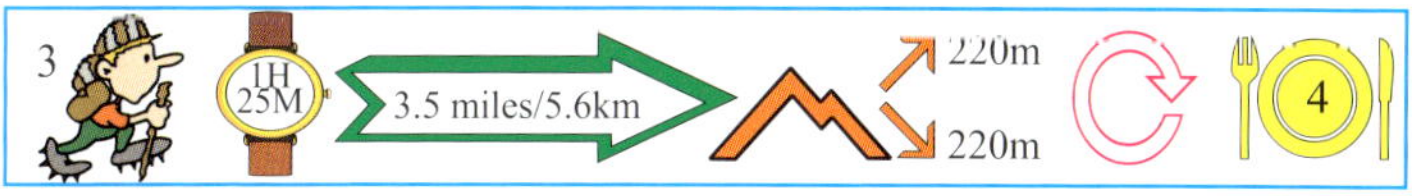

Access by car:

From junction 7 of the M5 head towards **Worcester**. At the first roundabout turn left and follow signs for the A449 first for 'Malvern' then 'Great Malvern'. Continuing on the A449 through **Great Malvern**, we first look out for the village sign for 'Malvern Wells' then **The Railway Inn** on the right and **Peachfield Road** on the left. Next on the right is **Eaton Road**, a quiet residential cul de sac which runs diagonally uphill; park on the left by a wall just before the end of it. OS Grid reference: SO 77199 43184 Nearest postcode: WR14 4PG.

Access by bus:

As with Walk 17, we could take bus N°362 or 363 which run every 30 minutes from **Great Malvern** to the bottom of **Eaton Road** (not Sun). The mile long walk from the town centre, much of it beside the common, is a pleasant alternative

At the end of **Eaton Road** we find a wooden Public Bridleway signpost (Wp.1 0M) and follow it up a tarmac and mud track (S). Passing to the right of a house, a well trodden path takes us steadily up through woodland, following

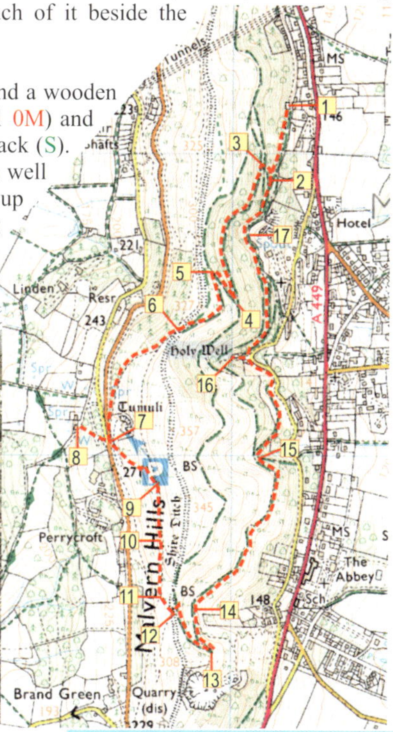

.. a well-trodden path ..

Walk 15 but taking a slightly different route up to the ridge. After keeping right at a fork we turn sharp right at the next junction (Wp.2 5M NW), heading up to meet a path that runs along the contour (Wp.3 7M) with a concrete sign to 'Holywell' embedded in a brick surround to our left and a bench to the right.

Our way is across it and to the left (ESE) but where Walk 15 goes right, we carry straight on, steadily maintaining the same gradient until, still in woodland, we take an acute right (Wp.4 13M NW). After a couple of minutes an acute left (Wp.5 15M S) enables us to maintain this gradient, taking us around to the right (SW) and out of the trees to attain the ridge opposite a clump of conifers. Here we go left, rejoining Walk 15 which has come around the base of **Jubilee Hill**.

In front of us there's a steep climb up **Pinnacle Hill**. Instead, we fork right (Wp.6 21M) and almost immediately right again (SW) to descend, now on **Malvern Hill's** western flank to **Gardiner's Quarry**, now a car park (Wp.7 28M). **The Kettle Sings**, an innocuous single storey brick building in an outstanding location, is across the road (WNW) further down the hill (Wp.8 30M). Its outside terrace, reached by going around to the right of the building, is a favourite.

Refreshed, we return to cross the road and pass through another limb of the car park further to the right. There we find another well-defined path climbing steadily at an angle to the right by a 'Have you paid and displayed?' sign (SE). It hairpins left (NE) and right (SE) by a bench before arriving at four steps that take us up onto a path that runs along the contour (Wp.9 38M).

Looking towards British Camp

We turn right (S) and start descending gently enjoying magnificent views of **British Camp** ahead. Ignoring a minor path up to the left (Wp.10 40M), we go down a little more steeply to reach a crossroad of tracks (Wp.11 44M) and turn left (SE) to cross the ridge with **Bredon Hill** prominent ahead beyond the **Severn** and **Avon** (Wp.12 46M).

We now descend on a smaller path, first swinging left (NE) then hairpinning right (SE); it's gently down through woodland to emerge with a view of **Upper Welland** just before reaching one of the many attractive paths that run along the contour (Wp.13 50M). Turning sharp left (NW), we stride easily along, our onward route visible around the hill far ahead. Another path joins us from the right (Wp.14 53M) and we begin to sweep further around to the right (NE), between steeply rising scrub-covered slopes to our left and gorse-covered downhill slopes to the right. Buzzards are often seen wheeling here in the warm air. As the path sweeps back left (NW) the Victorian buildings of **Great Malvern** come into view. The artificially squared-off area to our right is the **Three Counties Showground**.

Swinging back right again (N), we enter woodland and come to a meeting of ways (Wp.15 63M) with paths heading left and right but we carry on, slightly to the right (NE) and gently downhill. We swing right and left (N) before reaching a lane opposite a black and gold painted gas lamp where, rather than taking the footpath straight across, we go left (NW) and steadily up the lane to **Holywell Spring** (Wp.16 69M).

Holywell Spring

It's worth sampling the water; in the 18th century its supposed health giving properties made it the most important spring in the area. Then in the 1820s **St Ann's Well** became more popular, reinforced by the visit of Princess Victoria who became queen in 1831.

.. easy walking through beautiful woodland ..

We go left after leaving the building, guided by a green bridleway sign (NE) again walking on the flat along the contour. We ignore paths to left and right by a green metal bench as we follow our path a little to the left (N). It's easy walking through beautiful woodland with plenty of benches. Very pleasant!

A path back down to our right leads to another potential stop for tea at the **Cottage in the Wood Hotel** from which magnificent views can be enjoyed. Alternatively, we follow the wooden paling fence on our right which defines the hotel's boundary and at a choice of ways (Wp.17 78M), fork right to continue on the flat, then almost immediately fork left which takes us back onto our outward route (Wp.2 80M) where it's steadily down to our start (Wp.1 85M).

HEREFORDSHIRE BEACON from CASTLEMORTON COMMON

The **Herefordshire Beacon** (also called **British Camp**) is by far the most climbed, even though it's only the third highest of the **Malvern Hills** summits. And with good reason, as this substantial hill fort makes a splendid vantage point. We avoid the obvious route up from the large car park, starting instead across **Castlemorton Common** then up through woods to visit **Clutter's Cave** and **Millennium Hill** before reaching the top. Then it's down to the **Malvern Hills Hotel**, around **British Camp Reservoir** and back across the common to the **Plume of Feathers** to enjoy one of its splendid collection of real ales.

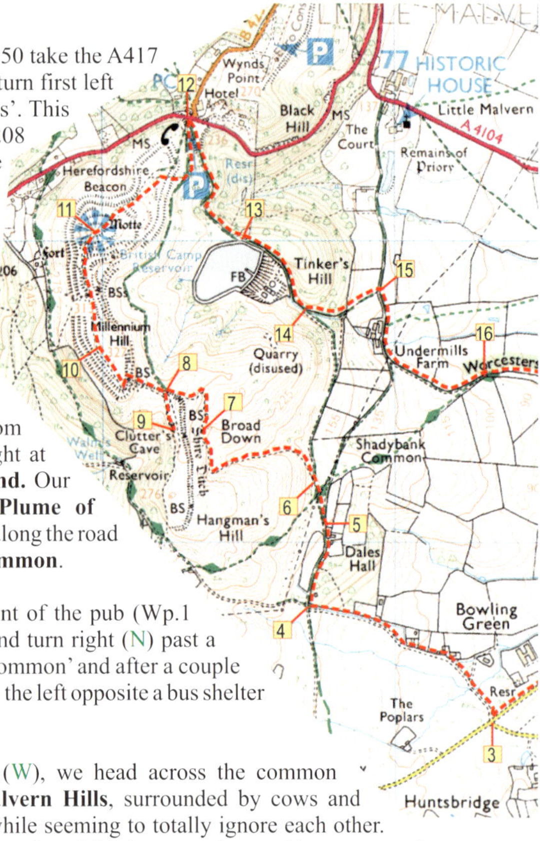

Access by car:
From junction 2 of the M50 take the A417 towards **Gloucester** and turn first left signposted 'The Malverns'. This minor road joins the B4208 and after crossing the A438, pass the **Robin Hood Inn** before parking on the right in front of the **The Plume of Feathers**. OS Grid reference: SO 78683 38804 nearest postcode: WR13 6JB.

Access by bus:
Take bus N°362 or 363 from **Great Malvern** and alight at **The Pheasant** in **Welland. Our** starting point of **The Plume of Feathers** is an easy mile along the road across **Castlemorton Common**.

From the car park in front of the pub (Wp.1 0M) we cross the road and turn right (N) past a sign for 'Castlemorton Common' and after a couple of minutes reach a lane on the left opposite a bus shelter (Wp.2 2M).

Turning down the lane (W), we head across the common straight towards the **Malvern Hills**, surrounded by cows and sheep grazing together while seeming to totally ignore each other. The strip of tarmac looks as though it's been put down with no preparation, a grey interloper in this unusual landscape of tussocky grass, interspersed with gorse, bramble thickets and the occasional tree.

Ahead is the cleft in the ridge of summits going up to **Gullet Quarry** (visited in our Walk 22, Gullet Quarry and Midsummer Hill). After passing a lane on our left and an ivy-draped house on our right, we reach a second lane to the left (Wp.3 20M) where we turn right (NW) down a gravel track.

At a fork we go left towards the hills (WNW); it's surprising to pass so many dwellings hidden in the folds of the common as we start gently climbing, the common still on our left and mature oak woodland now on our right. Where the track swings right (Wp.4 30M N) a bridleway joins us from the left; we also spot a new house built in the woods. Further on, we pass another isolated house with ponds in its garden containing impressively tall flag irises. Reaching a fork in the track (Wp.5 34M) we go left, ignoring the footpath steeply up further left. At first we continue parallel with our sister track, then go to the left of a field while it goes right, now with bracken and trees to our right.

We look for and take a larger footpath on the left with a 'No Horse Riding on this Path' sign (Wp.6 38M NNW), steadily climbing through woods. As we climb, the path swings left (W) and where trees grow so closely overhead that there's not enough light for undergrowth to flourish, there may be sheep perversely sheltering under them though it's neither raining or baking hot; what they chew here for sustenance is a mystery. Later the path temporarily flattens as it swings back right (N) on a terrace, then it's steadily up again to reach a metal barrier (Wp.7 49M) positioned to prevent horses and cyclists coming this way.

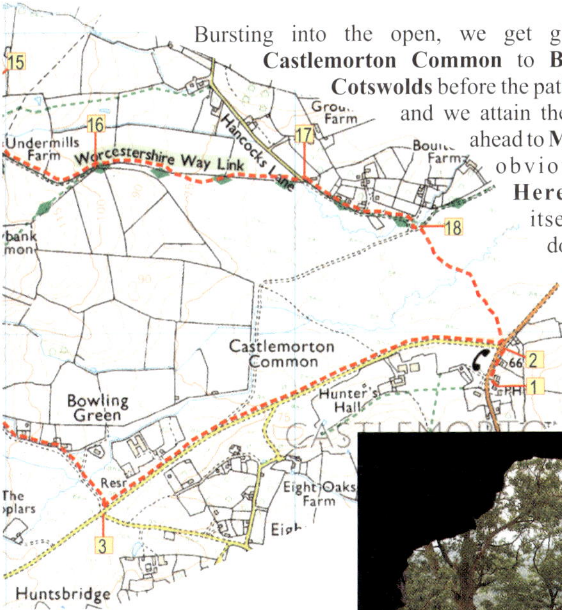

Bursting into the open, we get glorious views across **Castlemorton Common** to **Bredon Hill** and **The Cotswolds** before the path swings left again (W) and we attain the ridge. Here we look ahead to **Millennium Hill** and the obvious earthworks of **Herefordshire Beacon** itself before dropping down (WNW) to one of the circular toposcopes which are a feature of the hills (Wp.8 56M).

Clutter's Cave

Following the pointer left (SSE) we take a short detour to **Clutter's Cave** (Wp.9 60M), named after the hermit who lived here in the 18th century;

it's also known as **Giant's Cave** which, once you've seen it, seems inappropriate.

Retracing our steps (NNW), the views to our left across the series of wooded ridges to the **Welsh Marches** are particularly appealing. At the toposcope we go left (WNW) and begin to climb steadily. The Conservators have done an admirable job here by tastefully reinforcing the path and adding steps to limit the inevitable erosion on this busy route. Looking down to the right we see **British Camp Reservoir** which we'll skirt later then, after crossing the first set of earthworks, we swing right (NNW) and climb steadily up to the summit of **Millennium Hill** (Wp.10 69M).

Herefordshire Beacon

From here we enjoy views of **Herefordshire Beacon** with its multiple series of earthworks as we make our way along the well-walked path towards it (N). We climb past the second major set of defences before reaching the top where, surprisingly, there's no trig point and no obvious summit (Wp.11 78M); however it does provide the best view around.

The way down is obvious (NE) on a path even more substantially constructed than the one we followed on our route up. At a choice of steps right or a path straight on, we choose the steps to join the path encircling the beacon (N), descending steadily to a wooden gate and a vast car park (Wp.12 88M), though still not large enough on summer weekends despite the three pound charge. On the other side of the road is a kiosk selling sweets and ice creams beside the **Malvern Hills Hotel**.

At the far end of the car park we find a cattle grid beside a wooden barred gate and beyond, a tarmac track that takes us through woods (SSE). The track descends steadily with a steep drop to our left over a barrier and swings right then slowly left (SE) to arrive at a house with a chugging generator by the reservoir we spotted earlier (Wp.13 98M). After passing between the house and green railings 'protecting us' from the dangers beyond, it's steeply down on an unusual patterned concrete surface, swinging right (S) with woodland to our left.

British Camp Reservoir

After the track surface changes to gravel a stream joins us, clearly the outlet from the reservoir, and it's now steadily down beside a brick wall bulging from the weight of earth above.

Where the track divides (Wp.14 104M) we take the left hand, smaller option (E) which follows the stream, still steadily down but now perilously stony requiring careful footwork.

After the stream leaves us, we go through a rusty gate and out of the woods, following the contour to the left of an ancient tree across a field, to reach a stile by a metal barred gate (Wp.15 109M).

Undermills Farm

We head right (S) down a concreted track to **Undermills Farm** and its particularly attractive black and white farmhouse.

After the going changes to the 'more comfortable gravel with grass in the middle' variety, it veers left (ESE) and we gently climb to a metal barred gate, then keep left alongside the field edge. Now it's gently down again and getting closer to a fence on our right, we move across to walk alongside it (Wp.16 120M E) to a modern metal gate, then down a sunken way through scrubby woodland until we emerge into **Castlemorton Common** again.

After threading our way between somnolent cows we regain a gravel track to reach a ford and beside it, cross a plank bridge under a willow tree (Wp.17 130M). Here we turn right (ESE) into a lane beside dwellings scattered amid the common and swing right over a bridge (Wp.18 136M).

Our route across Castlemorton Common

The lane swings back left, then as vehicles come into view on a road across the common to our right, we make a beeline (SE) towards them; we're also heading in particular for the cream house with tall chimneys.

There's no path but we cross the tussocky grass between thistles and gorse and as we get closer, spot the bus shelter we passed at the beginning of the walk (Wp.2 144M). Reaching the road, we turn right (SW) and it's only a hop, skip and a jump back to the pub (Wp.1 146M).

20 CASTLEMORTON TUMP

As with Walk 19 (Herefordshire Beacon from Castlemorton Common), we start out from **The Plume of Feathers** in the heart of **Castlemorton Common** then for a change, head away from the **Malvern Hills** and across fields to **Castlemorton Church** and the Motte and Bailey behind it - **Castlemorton Tump**. It then continues east with glorious views south before returning along quiet, leafy byways and a green lane.

Access by car:
From junction 2 of the M50, take the A417 towards **Gloucester** and turn first left signposted 'The Malverns'. This minor road joins the B4208 and after crossing the A438, pass the **Robin Hood Inn** before parking on the right in front of **The Plume of Feathers**. OS Grid reference: SO 78691 38778 Nearest postcode: WR13 6JB.

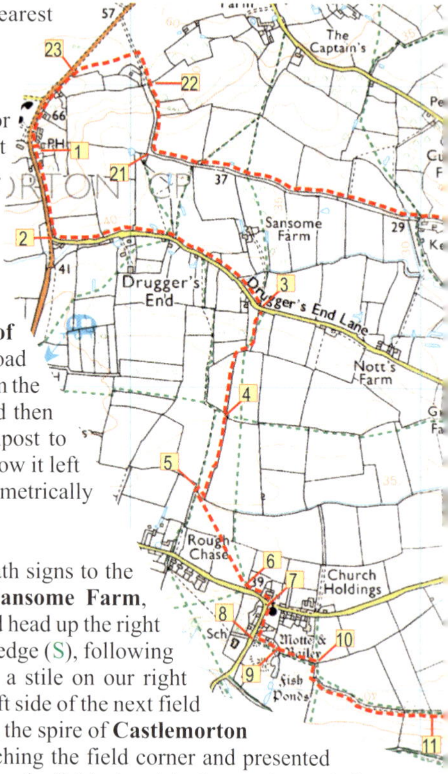

Access by bus:
As with Walk 19, take the Nº362 or 363 from **Great Malvern** and alight outside **The Pheasant** in **Welland.** Our starting point of **The Plume of Feathers** is an easy mile along the road across **Castlemorton Common**.

From the car park of **The Plume of Feathers** (Wp.1 0M) we cross the road and turn left and downhill (S), first on the pavement which fronts cottages and then on the grass verge. We spot a signpost to 'Druggers End' (Wp.2 4M) and follow it left (E) along an attractive, leafy lane diametrically away from the **Malvern Hills**.

We pass a couple of wooden footpath signs to the right but at the third, just after **Sansome Farm**, clamber over a stile (Wp.3 14M) and head up the right hand side of a field by a hawthorn hedge (S), following it right and left to reach and cross a stile on our right (Wp.4 21M). We go left down the left side of the next field with **Malvern Hills** to our right and the spire of **Castlemorton Church** poking up to the left. Reaching the field corner and presented with an impenetrable hedge we follow the field edge right then, as it goes left, find a stile hidden in the hedge (Wp.5 26M).

We now luxuriate in a meadow populated with dandelions and buttercups as we head towards the church (SE). A gap in the hedge takes us into the next field and thence to emerge, over a stile (Wp.6 31M), into a lane where we go left (ESE) into the village of **Castlemorton** itself.

Castlemorton Tump

While passing the church (Wp.7 33M) it's interesting to ponder why there's a ladder up the side of its spire. We turn right (SSW) down another lane, then opposite the primary school (Wp.8 35M) it's left through a metal gate where an excellent information board describes **Castlemorton Tump**, a motte and bailey castle laid out before us.

After exploring we make for the top of a waymark post just visible above a hummock to our left (ESE) and find that it's attached to a bridge sandwiched between metal gates (Wp.9 39M). We go on through one metal gate then another and to the left of a five barred gate (Wp.10 41M), where it's immediately right (S). We ignore another metal gate which would take us down a slope, to head left (ESE) along a small ridge beside a newly planted hawthorn hedge, following waymark posts.

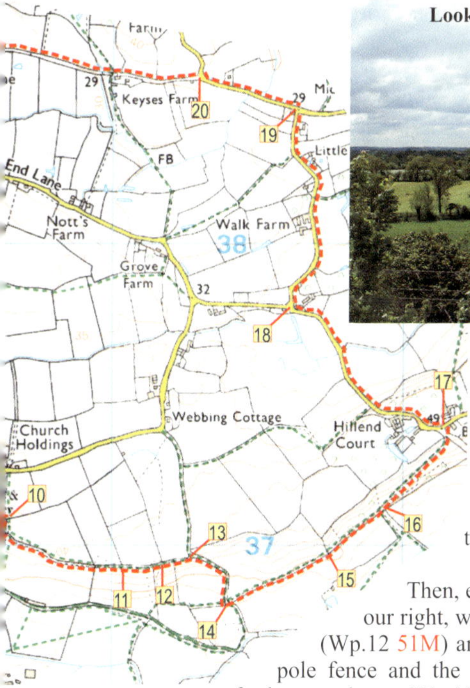

Looking towards Tewkesbury

Continuing along this ridge we go through a metal gate to the right of a wooden barred gate (Wp.11 49M) and stop to look to the right over **Miller's Court** towards **Tewkesbury** and back to **Castlemorton Church**.

Then, eschewing a stile in the hedge to our right, we go through another metal gate (Wp.12 51M) and find ourselves confined by a pole fence and the continuing hawthorn hedge. A further metal gate (Wp.13 53M) takes us down to meet a red clay farm track, reminiscent of those in Devon, where we turn right (SE) and go steeply down the slope which hitherto we've avoided. Where the farm track swings right into a field we carry straight on down to meet a rusty five barred gate (Wp.14 57M). There are three ways here; ours is the least obvious, up the bank to our left and over a stile where we first follow the field edge to our right, then make our way left (NE) between two crops heading across towards the right hand corner of a wood.

Dinking left and right, we enter the wood (Wp.15 63M) and tramp contentedly through its tranquil space. Too soon a gravel track joins us from the right (Wp.16 67M) and now it's upward, still through woodland, until we pass through a heavy metal gate (Wp.17 72M) to meet a lane. Here it's left (W) past **Hillend Court** which in addition to being a farm, seems to have grain processing capability. Now heading back towards the **Malvern Hills** we appreciate their full extent before a lane appears on our right with a signpost indicating 'Longdon Heath' and 'Upton upon Severn' (Wp.18 82M). We follow it (N) noticing a bank of gorgeously yellow cowslips to our right.

.. a particularly splendid cottage ..

Passing **Walk Farm** on our left, we spot a black and white farmhouse hidden behind a motley collection of outbuildings of various ages, before stopping to admire a particularly splendid cottage on the right, well-maintained without being fussily manicured.

The map informs us that we're in **Little Welland** but we've seen no signposts to it - perhaps this little gem would prefer not to be found. At a T junction (Wp.19 92M) we go left (W) signposted to 'Welland' and where the lane swings right (Wp.20 96M) it's straight on past an electricity sub-station. Then after **Keyses Farm** our way becomes a muddy track; be prepared to be startled by the clatter of ducks taking off from a weed-clogged pond complete with half-submerged boat.

After the track swings right (Wp.21 113M) we begin to climb (N), now in a sunken lane then, just beyond a wooden barred gate (Wp.22 116M) we emerge onto **Castlemorton Common** again with the twin peaks of **Worcestershire Beacon** and **North Hill** straight ahead. Here we go left (W) to meet a road at the sign for **Castlemorton** (Wp.23 120M) and then left again (SW) to arrive back at **The Plume of Feathers** (Wp.1 124M).

21 EASTNOR PARK

Here's a delightful, gentle stroll that skirts **Midsummer Hill** then climbs to the landmark obelisk in **Eastnor Park** before descending to **Eastnor** village. Field and woodland paths drop us close to **Ledbury** and a charming back route through the town to **The Market House**. Note that as this is a linear route and buses back to **Hollybush** are few and far between, a taxi from the rank opposite **The Market House** is the best bet.

Access by car:
From junction 2 of the M50 follow the A417 to **Ledbury t**own centre and at the traffic lights turn right onto the A449 signposted 'Malvern'. Out of the town fork right onto the A438 to **Tewkesbury** through **Eastnor** village. After passing the village sign for 'Hollybush' park on the left in a muddy car park at the foot of **Midsummer Hill**. OS Grid reference: SO 75878 36876 Nearest postcode: WR8 1ET.

Access by bus or train:
The best option is to walk the route in reverse, getting to **Ledbury** either by train (though the station is a distance from town) or by bus N°675 from **Great Malvern**.

From the car park (Wp.1 0M) it's over a stile by a cattle grid to start steadily up a tarmac track (NW) amid a clamour of birdsong with **Midsummer Hill** to our right. After swinging right (N) the tarmac changes to black grit and a view opens up to our left down to **Brewer's Cottage** and across **Eastnor Park**; now we get our first view of the imposing obelisk. The way flattens before we pass **Castle Copse Cottage** - what an exercise in alliteration - then it's gently up again to come over a rise and see **Swinyard Hill** ahead. Next we drop gently down passing through a metal barred gate (Wp.2 17M) by plentiful gorse before swinging steadily left (NW) with views between the **Malverns** to **Castlemorton Common**.

The Obelisk

Dropping down to a meeting of ways (Wp.3 20M) (acutely right is the way up from **Gullet Quarry**, explored in Walk 22), we go straight on (WSW) through a kissing gate to the right of a cattle grid and then take the middle of the three alternatives, through a metal barred gate then up a wide, well-worn track. A great view greets us along the valley to our left as we steadily climb but now have to pass the recently-fenced obelisk to the right and note the 'Falling Masonry - Please Keep Out' signs (Wp.4 27M). The impressive structure, visible from miles around, was erected in 1812 in memory of Edward Charles Somers, killed at the siege of Burgos.

Continuing, we begin dropping gently down (W), crossing a track (Wp.5 34M) and enjoying the view to the right all along the line of The Malverns. Now dropping more steeply, there's a wood to our right, bracken with a few hawthorns to our left and a pair of lakes ahead in the valley.

The lake in Eastnor Park

Right of a wooden barred gate (Wp.6 45M), we continue down the track to a T junction and here carry straight on across grass, following no visible path but making for a red lifebelt at the lake's edge. We head left beside the water, between the two lakes (Wp.7 51M) and across a wooden bridge.

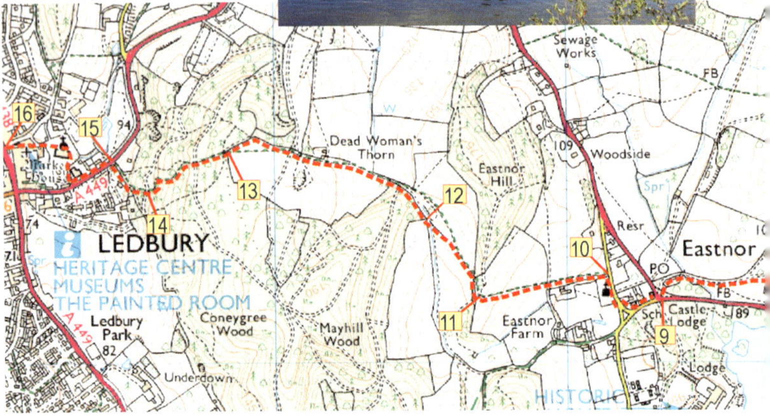

There we turn left (SSW), keeping a judicious distance from the water as the ground can be soggy, to walk down the valley, now entirely on the flat. To our left, the small stream has cut a surprisingly large cleft as it wends its way to **Eastnor Lake**. Coming upon a track (Wp.8 60M), we follow it right (W) through parkland where isolated old trees are interspersed with young trees protected from being nibbled by deer. We're now close to a main road; after passing **Eastnor Bowling Club** we join a tarmac track heading towards it.

Eastnor Church

Meeting the main road (Wp.9 67M) opposite the entrance to **Eastnor Castle**, we cross it into a quiet lane to the right of the castle, which leads to **Eastnor** village. In the centre of the village green we take a peek at an ornate drinking fountain before going right (NNW) keeping **Eastnor Church** on our left.

Beyond the church, at a public footpath sign (Wp.10 71M) we turn left (W) to the right of a metal fence and climb log steps up to a football pitch, then go left to walk beside it. Continuing in the same direction, we join a track that climbs steadily between fields. As the incline eases we swing right (Wp.11 80M NW) ignoring another track even further to the right to drop gently down through woods. But not for long, as soon we're out into another field making for a metal barred gate with a frustratingly difficult catch (Wp.12 84M) which takes us into woodland.

Now it's steadily up a muddy, flinty track close to the edge of the wood bearing left (WNW) then down again in roller coaster fashion. Where the main track swings left we carry straight on and over a stile to the left of a metal barred gate to emerge into field again. A well-trodden path takes us along the right field edge and through a wooden barred gate, past an area on our right intriguingly described on the map as **Dead Woman's Thorn**.

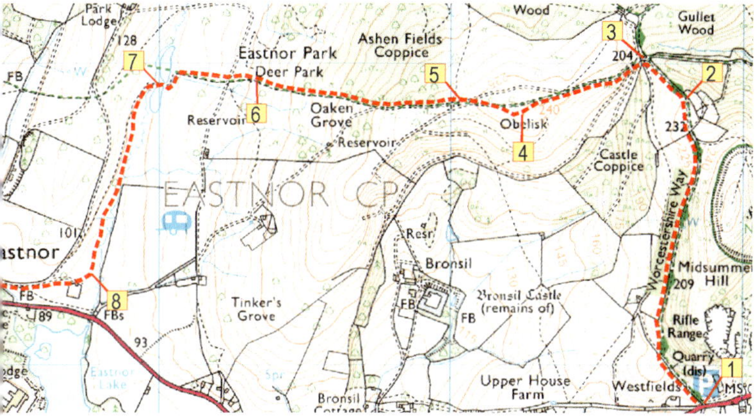

Ignoring a path to our right down into the wood, we continue slightly left (WSW) along the field edge to its corner (Wp.13 97M), then plunge down into woods and through an ancient, decrepit wooden gate with celandine underfoot. Straight across a fire break, we head down steps following a waymark on a way like a narrow sunken lane; it feels like we are following in the footsteps of many a weary traveller soon to have the chance of rest in **Ledbury**. The path swings left and right, becoming quite steep and reminiscent of a bobsleigh run before we cross a track (Wp.14 103M) where again there are steps down, this time with a helpful handrail.

Passing between gateposts and swinging right (WNW) with the path becoming wider, we go down shallow steps to suddenly meet a busy road (Wp.15 105M). Crossing it, steps take us up to a footpath where we walk left (WSW) beside a wall.

Immediately after the police station we turn right (N) into a narrow lane; thankfully it's quiet again as we make our way to **St. Michael's and All Angels' Church** and go around it to the right to find that church and tower are, surprisingly, separate.

Passing between church and tower

We pass between them (W) and out through the churchyard, an attractive walled garden to our right and **Abbot's Lodge** to our left as we fork left into the delightful, cobbled alleyway of **Butcher's Row** and pass **Ledbury Heritage Centre** and **Butcher's Row Folk Museum** before arriving at **The Market House** in the centre of **Ledbury** (Wp.16 115M).

Butcher's Row

Before leaving, we suggest sampling some of the many refreshment opportunities the town has to offer. We particular liked **Ceci Paolo**, an upmarket café above a cook shop and delicatessen by the traffic lights and **Mrs Muffin's,** a more traditional tea shop we passed in **Butcher's Row**.

For our return there are a few buses (Tourist Information is on 01531 636147), otherwise there's a taxi rank opposite **The Market House**.

22 GULLET QUARRY & MIDSUMMER HILL

From the car park below **Swinyard Hill**, our route goes up past the dramatic, water-filled **Gullet Quarry** as far as the **Malvern Hills** ridge, then further up to **Midsummer Hill** before dropping steeply down the other side to **Hollybush**, then gently down to a delightful mill pond in the **Golden Valley**. Finally, a meander across **Castlemorton Common** brings us to **Robin Hood Inn** for refreshments before returning along a quiet lane.

Access by car:
From junction 2 of the M50 take the A417 towards **Gloucester** and turn first left signposted 'The Malverns'. This minor road joins the B4208; on reaching **Castlemorton Common**, pass first the **Robin Hood Inn** and then **The Plume of Feathers**, before taking a turn into a lane on the left which takes us across the common to **Swinyard Car Park**. The £3 parking charge goes towards the upkeep of the **Malvern Hills**. OS Grid reference: SO 76640 38127, nearest postcode: WR13 6BX.

Shorter Version
(4.7 miles/7.5 km)
Miss out part of the meander across **Castlemorton Common** and the pub stop by continuing straight on at Wp.13 to Wp.17 where going left rejoins the main route.

Access by bus:
Take bus N°362 or 363 from **Great Malvern** and get off outside **The Pheasant** in **Welland**, then walk along the road across **Castlemorton Common**, reaching **Robin Hood Inn** soon after passing **The Plume of Feathers**; this is Wp.16.

From **Swinyard Car Park** (Wp.1 0M) we continue up the lane (W) with **Swinyard Hill** towering above us. Almost immediately this lane swings left but we carry straight on along a lane with a 'No Through Road - Residents and Emergency Vehicles Only' sign, passing **Ruffz** refreshment kiosk, reminiscent of a continental wayside bar.

Gullet Quarry

Bluebells, cowslips and forget-me-nots abound as we carry on up this cleft between **Midsummer** and **Swinyard Hills**. After passing a wayside cottage and a sign for 'Gullet Quarry' we reach a recently constructed stone wall, over which we view the stunning quarry site with a great cliff to the right and deep, forbidding water below us. Following the obvious way to the left, we pass a Gullet Quarry information board (Wp.2 7M) noting its dire warnings against climbing the cliffs or swimming in the quarry and walk along beside the water remarking on the myriad reflections.

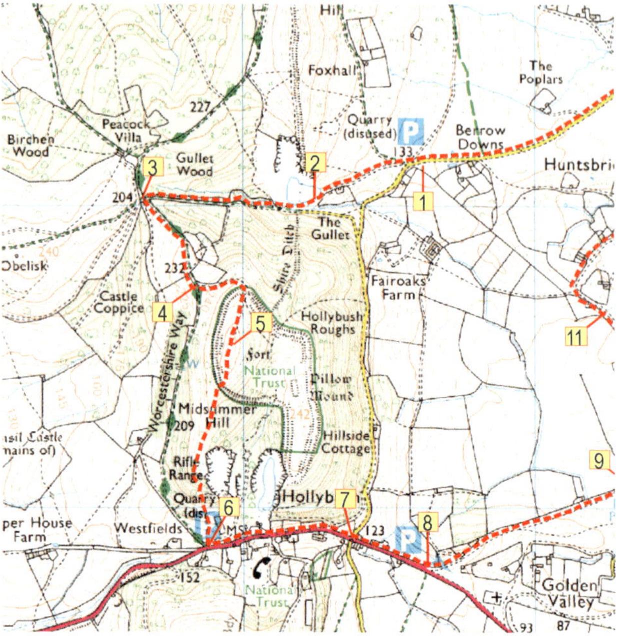

Beyond the quarry, a track joins us from the left. There are several ways forward; ours is the waymarked rocky track between posts. Now it's steadily up through woodland to a meeting of the ways (Wp.3 17M) where we turn sharp left (SE) onto a gravel track, still climbing steadily and still with woods to our left but now with open views across **Eastnor Park** to the right.

Bluebells on Midsummer Hill

After the track swings right (SSE) and flattens we go through a new metal barred gate and the woods give way to an isolated property nestling in a fold of the contour - what a view they must have! We turn left off the main track (Wp.4 23M) to follow a footpath up **Midsummer Hill** (E) with stunning bluebells forming a blue carpet to our right as we climb steadily.

Looking back, there's a beautiful view over a succession of ridges to the west and we pick out the distinctive shape of **Hay Bluff**. Beginning a long sweep to the right, first the view left is north of **Swinyard Hill**, **Hangman's Hill** and **Herefordshire Beacon**, then east steep down and right across the **Severn Plain**. After passing a National Trust sign, we climb up between banks (SSW) before approaching the summit (Wp.5 34M) on a gentle grass path. The 360° view from here is second to none - such a shame that an ugly concrete shelter, even though it now has in information board attached, spoils the general feeling of well-being engendered here.

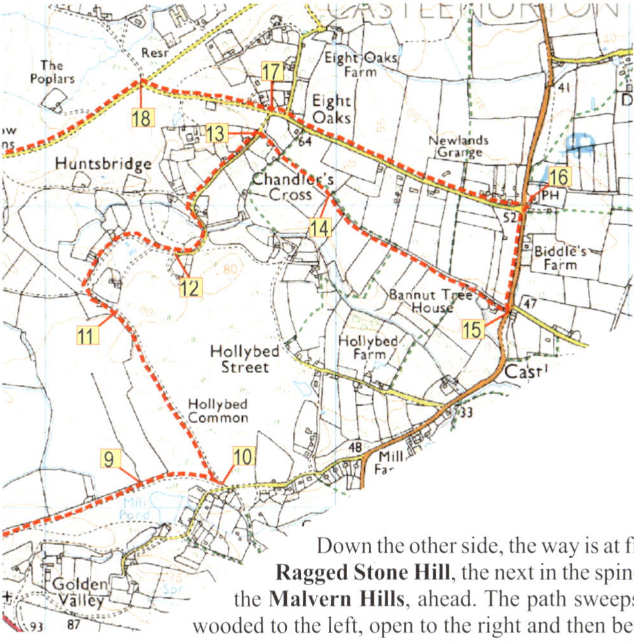

Down the other side, the way is at first grassy, with **Ragged Stone Hill**, the next in the spine that makes up the **Malvern Hills**, ahead. The path sweeps right and left, wooded to the left, open to the right and then becomes gravelly and slippery as it plunges steep down through woodland with some convenient trees ready to be clung to if our progress gets out of control. We pass between brambles before reaching a grassy area but it's still steep down until we reach a metal gate with the car park at **Hollybush** (from which Walks 21 and 23 start) on the other side (Wp.6 48M).

Crossing the main road we walk along the pavement to the left (E) beside a thatched cottage reminiscent of a picture from a story book and, now steadily down, we pass a phone box and **Berrow House** camp site before reaching a crossroads (Wp.7 54M). Here it's straight on (ESE) past **Hollybush Church Rooms**, now on a narrow grass verge beside a ditch (ESE) until we come to a grassy car park on the left (Wp.8 58M). Leaving the road (ENE) we go to the left of the cars and to the right of **Bank Cottage** with a friendly looking dragon sculpture in its garden, then carry on in the same direction with a great view over **Golden Valley** within the larger area of **Castlemorton Common**.

Following the green swathe, we fork left and make for the left hand edge of the **Mill Pond** where we pass between boulders placed to restrict cars coming from the other direction, to reach an idyllic spot for children to play (Wp.9 71M) with its benches, large grass area and pond where ducks clamour to be fed.

Mill Pond

Continuing in a similar direction (E) on a gravel track, we head towards some scattered dwellings but when we meet tarmac (Wp.10 77M) turn very sharp left away from it (NW) opposite a cottage named 'The Homestead', back towards the hills on a grass track heading for a 'Walkers and Horse Riders Only Beyond this Point' sign.

Here, revelling in the easy walking, we enjoy stunning views all along the hills in front of us. Our way takes us between two posts and then between two further posts to a red-tiled cottage with its garden enclosed by a hedge (Wp.11 86M). Veering left takes us around its boundary (WNW) on a stony track with a cream cottage to our left and after the track turns right (NE) we come upon a farmhouse. The track swings further right (E) by an orchard and where it meets another track (Wp.12 92M) can realistically be described as a lane, which swings left (NNW) and right (NE) through this unusual landscape of properties scattered amidst common land.

Eventually, we reach a house on the right (Wp.13 101M) turning right (SE) down the track with grass in the middle that runs beside it; if we reach a T junction of lanes, only fifty metres further on, we've gone too far! Where this track sweeps right to a second house, we keep straight on though a gap in a fence along a footpath to a stile. Now it's up the right hand edge of a succession of fields (not well-trodden and amid buttercups and daisies) that are successively separated by a rusty metal gate tied up with string (Wp.14 108M), a rickety, wooden gate, a stile and finally, a further rusty gate which takes us into a grassy lane with woodland on the left and a hedge on the right. After a series of buildings on the right we cross a cattle grid to reach a road by a magnificent horse chestnut tree (Wp.15 118M), here it's left (N) passing **Biddles Farm** and **The Old Smithy** to reach the **Robin Hood Inn** (Wp.16 123M).

.. sheep wander ..

Opposite **The Old Smithy** we find a lane which leads us gently upwards (WNW) as sheep wander inconsequentially about. After a lane to the right we come to another on the left (Wp.17 136M) where the shorter version of this walk joins us, and pass a pond down to our right before meeting open common land with bracken, hawthorn trees and gorse.

We pass another pond, this time surrounded by willow trees. In front of a farm we reach a T junction (Wp.18 143M) where we turn left (WSW) onto another lane which takes us past a large green space, ideal for impromptu games. The gradient increases slightly, then we are back at the car park (Wp.1 153M).

23 RAGGED STONE AND CHASE END HILLS

Though one of the shortest walks in the book, it's not an easy stroll as it includes two stiff climbs and a very steep descent. It scales the two most southerly of the **Malvern Hills** summits starting from the car park in **Hollybush** (used in Walk 21) and visits the charming hamlet of **Whiteleaved Oak** which nestles between them.

Access by car:
From junction 2 of the M50 follow the A417 to **Ledbury** town **c**entre and at the traffic lights turn right onto the A449 signposted 'Malvern'. Out of the town, fork right onto the A438 to **Tewkesbury** through **Eastnor** and, after passing the village sign for 'Hollybush' park on the left in a muddy car park at the foot of **Midsummer Hill**. OS Grid reference: SO 75894 36886 nearest postcode: HR8 1ET.

A LONGER VERSION
A longer walk to include an additional summit (and a pub stop) can be made by taking this route to Wp.11 then turning right down the road and following Walk 21 from its Wp.7 back past its start and over **Midsummer Hill** to the car park at its Wp.6.

Access by bus:
Although there's a bus stop opposite our starting point, buses stop here only twice a week. Let's hope this situation changes soon.

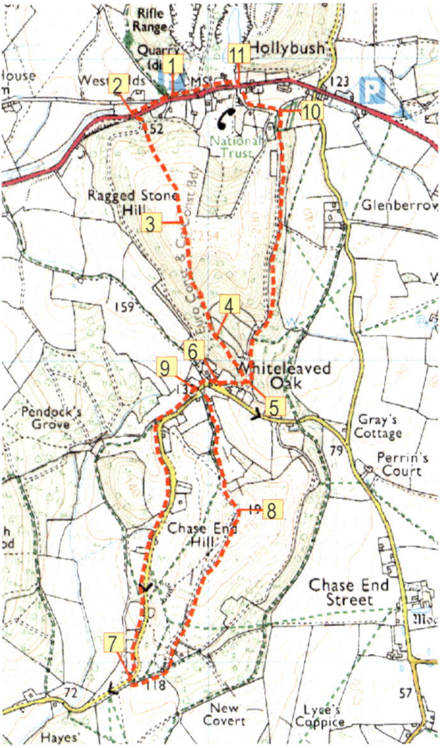

From the car park (Wp.1 0M) we cross the road and follow it down right (WSW) past a bus shelter that's seen better days until we reach a kissing gate beside a metal barred gate (Wp.2 2M) on the left. This takes us into woodland where we go left at a choice of ways (SSE) and climb steadily through overgrown bracken.

As it steepens we can look back to the obelisk in **Eastnor Park** (visited on Walk 20) and even before reaching the top of **Ragged Stone Hill** we have views across the **Severn Plain** to the east. Although we haven't climbed that far, the bracken is stunted compared to the virulent growth we've pushed past on our way up - perhaps it's just more exposed here.

Hollybush Quarry and Midsummer Hill

On reaching the summit (Wp.3 14M), we look back to **Hollybush** and **Midsummer Hill** before walking along the short ridge to descend the other side. First we go to the right of the ridge, then slightly left to join a larger path and go steeply down to the left of gorse bushes.

On top of Ragged Stone Hill

After this steep section our path changes to what feels like an ancient way with a gnarled hawthorn hedge accompanying us on the right.

An aged post (Wp.4 24M) with a waymark pinned to it confirms this impression and here we dink right to join an alternative path off the hill. The trig point of our second summit of **Chase End Hill** is visible straight ahead as we continue steadily down through woodland to join a much larger path (Wp.5 27M).

A cottage in Whiteleaved Oak

The larger path immediately swings right (W) and becomes a track leading down behind cottages through a wooden barred gate to a lane (Wp.6 29M). We go right then swing left (SW) through the hamlet of **Whiteleaved Oak** where several ley lines intersect; there's certainly a good feel here with its collection of attractive cottages.

The lane continues steadily down, swinging left again (S). We carry on along passing a lottery-funded cattle grid until we reach a cottage on the right with parking spaces to the left and a **Chase End Hill** information board (Wp.7 43M). To the left is a stile which would take us into **Bromsberrow Estate** but our way is more acutely left (ENE) to climb steadily up towards our second summit.

A waymark post indicates a choice of routes but the one to the left is so overgrown we choose to ignore it.

Whiteleaved Oak and Ragged Stone Hill

Then we pass an option to the right which goes though a wooden gate into a mass of rhododendrons while we continue up the broad grassy path (NE) with a good view of **Bredon Hill** to the right. Looking back we see the distinctive group of trees atop **May Hill**.

At a fork either path will do but we take the rightmost, lower alternative and before long spot the trig point marking the top of **Chase End Hill** a little to the left and make straight for it (Wp.8 54M).

Now we go steep, steep, steep down to the left (NW) on a grass path between rosebay willow herb with **Eastnor Castle** dead ahead.

Soon the path narrows and now only drops steadily before swinging right (NNW) and becoming a sunken lane. Reaching habitation, we pass **Cider Mill Cottage** before meeting the lane through **Whiteleaved Oak** again (Wp.9 61M). Turning right, we immediately swing right (E), retracing our steps and forking left onto a track (Wp.6 62M). This takes us back up through a wooden gate where we continue backtracking to circle left behind a cottage but where the footpath goes further to the left signposted 'Ragged Stone' (Wp.5 64M) we continue on a wide path through woods (N) with a steep drop to our right.

After ignoring a footpath to the left into a dell we follow along beside a fence on our right. A footpath on the right through a wooden barred gate looks enticing, but we carry on, now climbing steadily through woodland. A further path joins us from the right, young partridges scuttling hither and thither in front of us before we swing left (W) and a track joins ours with signs of human habitation again (Wp.10 76M). We pass an alternative path up to **Ragged Stone Hill** before going through a wooden barred gate and heading right (NW) down a track reinforced with concrete, to the main road (Wp.11 78M). We turn left (W) and it's back up the road to find our car behind the hedge on the other side of the road. (Wp.1 81M).

24 CRADLEY AND WEST MALVERN

From the church in **Cradley**, this walk takes us through fields and woodland to **West Malvern**. It then ascends to the ridge of **The Malverns** before running around the contour half way up **North Hill** on **Lady Howard de Walden Drive**, providing us with spectacular views down the chimney pots of **Great Malvern** and across the **Severn Plain**. Lunch is best taken at the café attached to **Elim Theological College** as both pubs in **West Malvern** are quite likely to be closed at lunchtime.

Access by car:
From junction 7 of the M5 head towards **Worcester**. At the first roundabout turn left and follow signs around the bypass (A4440) until turning left onto the A4103 signposted 'Hereford'. After passing through **Bransford** and **Leigh Sinton**, turn left to **Cradley** opposite a garage and in the village, turn left at the war memorial and park by a wall adjoining the church. OS Grid reference : SO 73533 47110 Nearest postcode : WR13 5LH.

Access by bus:
The only bus that goes to **Cradley** is the N°417 that runs between **Worcester** and **Ledbury**. If you're staying in **Great Malvern** an alternative is to walk up **Happy Valley** from the town centre to Wp.15 and start the circuit from there.

From the church (Wp.1 0M) it's back to the war memorial and left along the road for a few metres (S) but where it goes right we carry straight on along a stony track signposted 'Mathon'. This takes us past cottages and a waymark post offering us options of left, right or forwards; ours is forwards, first passing apple trees on our left then going gently down into open fields. The track swings slowly left (NE), then more sharply right (Wp.2 7M SE) and we begin to gently climb by a luxuriant hedge. Where the hedge ends we swing left (NE) towards some buildings, then right up to a metal barred gate (Wp.3 13M). After the gate we go right (S) following a waymark sign up by a hedge and slightly to the left to reach a gate opposite outbuildings of **Netherley Hall** (Wp.4 20M).

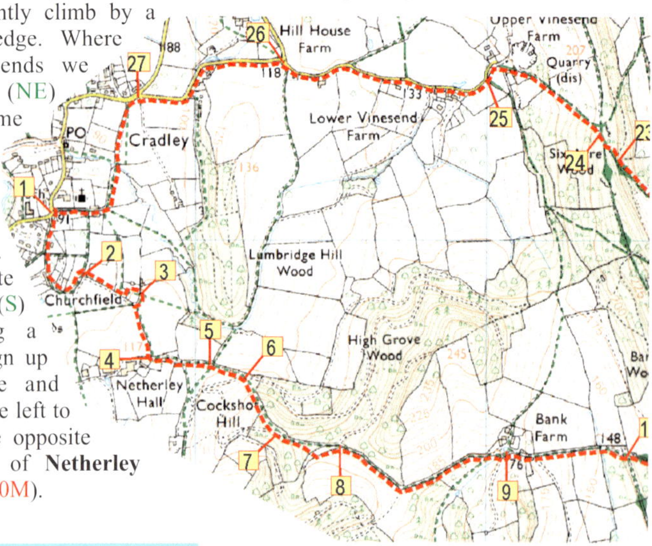

Netherly Hall

Our way is left (E) in front of a sturdy farmhouse along a track; presented with two metal barred gates we take the rightmost then fork left to continue in the same direction now towards woodland. At a metal barred gate (Wp.5 24M) we go to the right of it beside a fence, climbing gently until we spot a waymark nailed to a fence post.

This leads us steeply up to the right beside a depression, our route confirmed by another waymark pinned to a tree, and on to the corner of a wood. It's a surprisingly severe climb so it's a good idea to stop to take a breath and enjoy the view, encompassing **Cradley Church** and **Netherley Hall**.

Continuing up the side of the wood (SE), we come to a stile (Wp.6 31M) and enter the woods, thankfully now climbing only steadily. Before long we're over the top and go steadily down with a steep drop to our left until we reach a track (Wp.7 33M). Here we go left (ESE) and continue though the woods, passing another track that joins us on the left (Wp.8 37M). For a while we run along beside the woods but after swinging left (ENE), we leave their shelter, pass through two metal barred gates and descend steadily, accompanied by a row of mature oaks on our right

After a metal barred gate, our way becomes a tarmac track leading to **Bank Farm** (Wp.9 47M) where we follow the ribbon of tarmac right (E). Now going steadily down we see the houses of **West Malvern** across the valley then, after reaching the valley floor, start gently climbing again through trees. Where the lane swings right (Wp.10 53M) we go straight on over a stile and follow a delightful footpath up through woods and into a field. Now there's no obvious footpath, but we carry on in the same direction, going steadily upwards to a tall waymark post. This points slightly to the right and we follow it steadily upward to find a further waymark post and a track which takes us right (SE) along the contour with great views across the valley.

Now we're on the flat; before long another waymark post (Wp.11 61.M) points left and although there's no sign of a path, we follow its direction (E) as we spot a stile at the field edge.

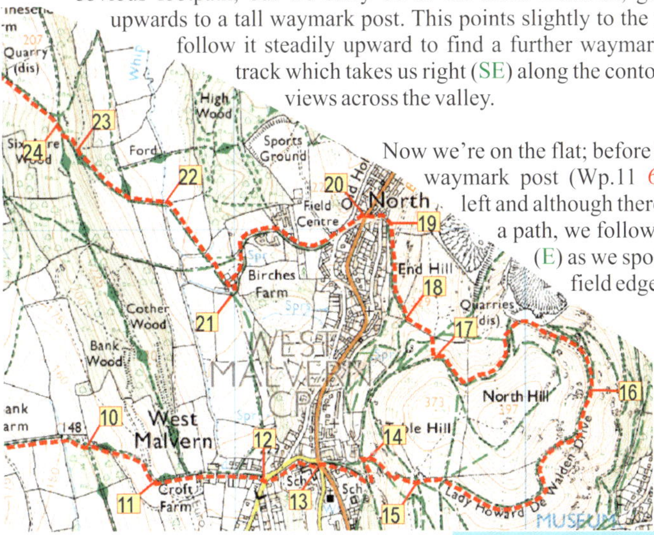

After two stiles, the second to the right of a metal barred gate, we carry straight on through the detritus of **Croft Farm** and past a duck pond, into a residential lane. On reaching a road (Wp.12 68M), we turn left and go steadily up, the beginning of our climb to the ridge of **The Malverns**. Ignoring **Mathon Road** to the left, **Croft Bank** takes us steeply up to **West Malvern Road** (Wp.13 72M) where we go straight across. Spotting an ice cream sign, we follow it to a pleasant café attached to a theological college, with a choice of indoor or outdoor seating,. After our break we go up **Westminster Bank**, passing **Bank House** where the tarmac ends. Continuing up to the right would take us to **Worcestershire Beacon** but we go sharp left (N) towards a Victorian weathervane (Wp.14 78M), where we turn right (ESE) by a bench with a great position to sit and look back at where we've come from.

Following a concrete signpost indicating 'Great Malvern' it's steep up again, first between bracken and masses of rosebay willow herb, then zigzagging between trees. Once out of the trees we soon reach a meeting of ways (Wp.15 85M) where the ridge extends away to our right up to **Worcestershire Beacon** and beyond.

Lady Howard de Walden Drive

Our way is now left, then steep down to the right (E) heading for the wide gravel path of **Lady Howard de Walden Drive** straight ahead, a magnificent Victorian construction which runs around the contour to the east of **North Hill**, providing us with breath taking views across **Great Malvern**. There are plenty of spots to stop; recommended is a rock that juts out right above the town. The path swings gently around to the left (N) before reaching a fork (Wp.16 99M) where we continue left (WNW), now looking down to **Malvern Link** and the railway line stretching away to **Worcester**.

Looking over Great Malvern

After going left at a further fork (SSW) our way is up away from the town with the land dropping steeply down on the right to **North Quarry**. We ignore a path steeply up to the left, instead turning right (NW) where a smaller path running from **North Hill** to the aptly named **End Hill** diagonally crosses us (Wp.17 115M). Dropping down, there are many intersecting paths but our way is to the left, steeply down the valley on a wide, grassy path to the left of **End Hill** (WNW) towards the houses of **West Malvern**. The path becomes steeper before we meet a track (Wp.18 118M) where we go right (NW) with buildings down to our left visible through trees. Ignoring paths to left and right, our descent lessens and the track dwindles to a path running behind cottages (N) and through a black metal gate (Wp.19 123M). We descend steep, makeshift steps to a lane (W) and **The Lamb** (Wp.20 125M).

After crossing the main road though the village we take **Old Hollow**, the lane opposite, and go straight across another road towards **Malvern Hills Outdoor Centre** (WSW). Dropping steadily, we swing right (NW) before passing the centre's offices, then slowly back left (S), particularly admiring the climbing towers among the plethora of activities available before reaching **Birches Farm** (Wp.21 136M). To the farm's left, we go over a metal barred gate then half right (NW) with a wooded ridge to our left. Across a field, we cross a stile beside a gate to continue down the valley, then in the corner of the next field go over a gate (Wp.22 141M), across a bridge and up the right hand edge of a field towards trees. The route is now through an open metal barred gate and along a faint track (WNW), following a bridleway sign steadily upward.

On entering **Six Acre Wood** our path becomes obvious - so often the way. We go though a gate (Wp.23 149M) where trees meet overhead. As we crest the ridge we meet a bridleway with plenty of evidence of passing horses, turn right (NW) onto it, then almost immediately go left (Wp.24 153M), steadily down the other side of the ridge. Ignoring a path to the left, our way descends more gently with a field, then a high hedge on our right. The path emerges onto a rough track and we go through a metal barred gate (Wp.25 162M) and swing left (W) into a lane.

This lane is delightful; with high hedges, almost no traffic and on the flat, we make good progress. After passing a footpath sign to 'Storridge' on the right, a similar sign to our starting point of 'Cradley' on the left seems tempting - we resist the temptation and immediately afterwards turn left down a tiny lane (Wp.26 173M) also signposted 'Cradley'.

.. unusual stile in a gate ..

Along this tunnel of greenery we pass a pond on the right and a further path off to the left before meeting the road (Wp.27 180M) that brought us to our starting point. Our way is left and almost immediately left again (SSW) over an unusual stile in a gate and along the right hand side of the field. After crossing a stream between two stiles, we go up the right hand field edge and at the top right (W) over a stile beside a metal barred gate to pass **Cradley Church** on the way back to our car (Wp.1 191M).

Cradley Church

25 OLD STORRIDGE COMMON

If you like woodland walks, then this one's for you - though don't think that because it's *not* on the **Malvern Hills**, there won't be any ups and downs either! The route starts outside the **Knapp and Papermill Nature Reserve** and climbs up through orchard and woodland over **Old Storridge Common** to lunch in **The New Inn** halfway between **Storridge** and **Leigh Sinton**. Return is back over the hill through **Birchwood**, finishing along **Leigh Brook** within the Nature Reserve.

N.B. It's a reflection of how wooded this walk is that GPS reception is poor Wp.2 to Wp.5, Wp.18 to Wp.20 and Wp.24 back to Wp.1.

Access by car:
From junction 7 of the M5 head towards **Worcester**. At the first roundabout turn left and follow its ring road around until reaching the A4103 to **Hereford**. In **Bransford** turn right at a roundabout signposted to 'Leigh, 'Alfrick' and 'Suckley' and shortly afterwards fork left towards **Suckley**. After a village sign for 'Alfrick Pound' and a lane to the left to 'Old Storridge'**,** park in one of the two lay-bys on the right opposite a post box. At busy times the gate to the field on the corner will be unlocked and can also be used for parking. OS Grid reference : SO 75099 52161 Nearest postcode : WR6 5HR.

Access by bus:
Our only suggestion is to use the N°417 that runs between **Ledbury** and **Worcester**, getting off at **The New Inn** (Wp.13) and doing the circuit from there.

From the lay-by (Wp.1 0M) we head back along the road, then go right (S) up a lane signposted to 'Old Storridge' where it's gently up between high hedges that sometimes meet to form a tunnel between a scattering of residential properties, mostly hidden behind trees. A wooden public footpath sign (Wp.2 6M) on the left points to our track that climbs more steeply to a stile beside a metal barred gate. After the stile we go immediately left into an orchard, then diagonally right (SE) to the left of a pond surrounded by a barbed wire fence. We follow the orchard's left hand boundary towards its top corner.

Old Storridge Common

On approaching the corner a stile comes into view in front of us (Wp.3 12M) where there are paths left, right and straight on. Ours is straight on, steadily upward through dense woods to meet a wider path that joins us from the right (Wp.4 15M).

From the gloom of the wood, a metal barred gate ahead (Wp.5

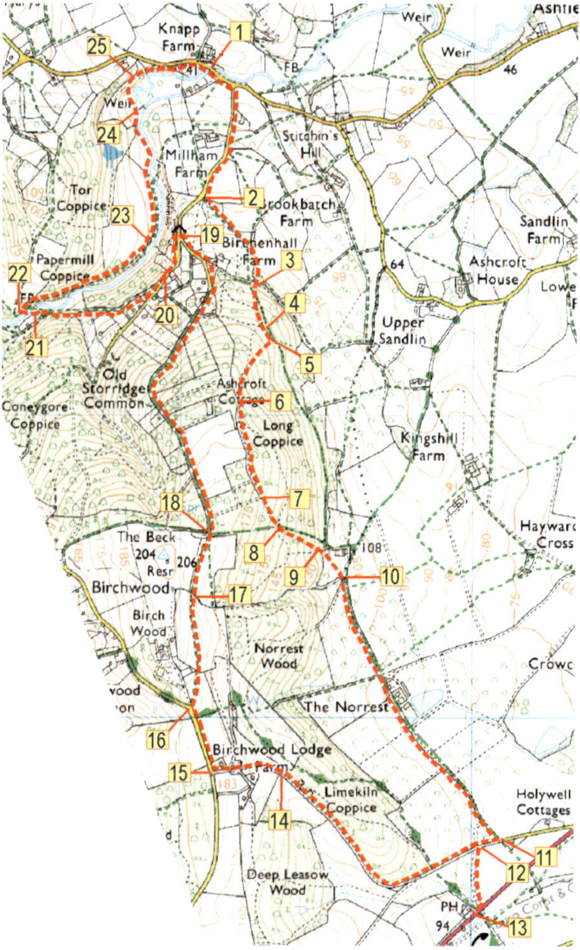

17M) glints in the sunlight and on reaching it the transformation to the sun drenched meadow land is extreme (on a sunny day of course). Swinging to the right, (SW) we go steeply up towards more trees - looking back, the view is magnificent!

Levelling off before we reach them, the path swings back to the left (S) to run along parallel to the woods before it divides (Wp.6 23M); here we take the right hand, narrower option through buttercups, white and purple clover and thistles back into the ever-present woodland.

For the first time today we find ourselves descending, first gently, with a fence to our right, a seemingly superfluous barrier, then more steeply to pass a metal gate on the right (Wp.7 28M) where another path joins us from further up the hill. Carrying straight on, we burst out of the wood again and push through bracken with **North Hill**, the Malvern's northernmost summit, starkly in front of us. As we descend, an ever widening panorama opens up. Soon we meet the path we split from at Wp.6 for our further foray into the woods; at a crossroad of paths (Wp.8 31M) we go left (SE), now steeply down with the staggering view omnipresent.

After a waymark under an oak tree, we fork right (Wp.9 34M) rather than go even more steeply downward and wind between bracken to reach a difficult-to-open metal gate (Wp.10 37M). Lifting it and pulling it towards oneself does the trick, enabling us to go right onto a track past a cereal crop and then orchards, now on the level, with **North Hill** still making its presence felt. Along this track we pass an attractive courtyard development on the left where the track becomes a proper tarmac lane before reaching a T junction (Wp.11 50M). Here it's right (WSW) onto a track, then left (S), following a public footpath sign (Wp.12 51M) along a grassy track towards a main-ish sounding road where **The New Inn** (Wp.13 55M), our lunch stop, is just to the right.

After our break we retrace our footsteps (N) back to the public footpath sign (Wp.12 60M) and turn left (WSW), gently up a beautiful, sun-dappled track through woodland.

North Hill from Birchwood

A footpath crosses ours, the stony surface underfoot interspersed with areas where years of leaf mould haven't been washed away, indicating an ancient way. The track swings to the right (NW) and narrows to a path, now with woodland to the right and an impenetrable hedge to the left which bars the view; on reaching a gate we can stop to enjoy it all the more.

Now its steadily up, and after a path joins us from within the murky wood, we come to a gate (Wp.14 74M) which takes us out into a field. Here it's straight on, up to a stile to the left of a gate, then up the left hand side of a field (W) beside the vegetable garden of a bungalow. At another gate it's straight on again between properties, one of which is **Birchwood Forge**, to reach a lane (Wp.15 78M). Turning right (N), we get a one-off chance to look across **Birchwood Common** through a gap in the hedge on the left before passing a footpath to the right. Then, where the lane swings left and a track goes straight on signed 'Birchwood Hall' and 'Anybodys Farm', we spot a gap in the hedge to the right and clamber over a stile (Wp.16 82M) to find ourselves in a field.

First we make for the corner of a wood to our left, then follow along the right side of a large field, heading for a distant cottage nestling at the edge of a further wood. At the corner of this field (Wp.17 88M) we find a gap into the next field and head across to the right of the cottage where a kissing gate (Wp.18 92M) takes us into sun-dappled woodland again. A well-used path drops down steeply to our right while we go straight on, following a grassy footpath by the cottage. The way becomes progressively more substantial and the gradient steeper as we pass a surprising number of properties hiding in the wood.

After ignoring several alternatives to left and right, we eventually reach a T junction of lanes (Wp.19 109M). Here we go acutely left (SSW), now on the flat, then where the lane starts climbing, we take a track slightly right (Wp.20 111M) with a 'No Vehicles Public Footpath Only' sign. This takes us gently down through more woodland, swinging to the right (W) where a footpath joins us down from the left, after which **Leigh Brook** can be heard burbling away below us. The track ends at a house where a sturdy wooden bridge (Wp.21 119M) takes us over what we fairly describe as a river into **Knapp and Papermill Nature Reserve**.

The only way is steeply up away from the river - but not for long, because at a kissing gate we turn sharp right (ENE) and at a further divide (Wp.22 121M) go right again through an open gate and down to follow along beside the river.

Not surprisingly it's a wee bit muddy, but at a wooden gate (Wp.23 129M) we pass out of the woods into pasture land and swing to the left (N).

There are several more gates and places where we can leave the main path to go closer to the river if we choose; we continue through this verdant environment abounding with birds and insects. Then, attracted by the sound of rushing water, we take a minor detour to a weir (Wp.24 137M) and find a fallen tree trunk which makes a great place for a stop.

Knapp and Papermill Nature Reserve

After a pair of wooden gates side by side (Wp.25 140M), we ignore steps down from the left and start climbing steadily upward swinging right (NE) above the river to reach a locked gate by a road. Our way is forward (E), following a 'Way Out' sign, to what looks like the back door into somebody's garden but through it find the **Worcester Wildlife Centre** building, where we sign the visitors book before making our way out past picnic benches and through a gate to meet the road where, to the right, our car awaits (Wp.1 145M).

26 COLWALL CHURCH, OYSTER HILL AND LEDBURY

From **Colwall Church**, we head away from **The Malverns** for a change and up the dome of **Oyster Hill** where we enjoy a different set of views westward, before continuing along field paths and through orchards, to the ancient market town of **Ledbury**. After lunching at one of its multitudinous choice of eateries, return is mostly through woodland, first by **Dog Hill**, where we follow the ancient packhorse route to **Worcester**, and then along a ridge through **Frith Wood**.

Access by car:
From junction 2 of the M50, follow the A417 to **Ledbury** town centre and at the traffic lights turn right onto the A449 signposted 'Malvern'. After starting the climb which would take us up and over **The Malverns**, turn left onto the B4218 to **Colwall** but shortly, where it turns right, go straight on signposted 'Coddington' and 'Wellington Heath'. Next it's right after going under a railway bridge, heading towards 'Coddington' and 'Mathon' along a tiny lane which comes out at a T junction by **Colwall Church**. Follow signs around to the left to its large car park. OS Grid reference : SO 73846 42271 Nearest postcode : WR18 6HE.

Access by bus or train:
This time we have several choices; we can take the train or bus N°675 from **Great Malvern** to **Colwall** and walk to the start at **Colwall Church** or continue on either vehicle to **Ledbury** (Wp.15 102M) and do the circuit from there. The N°675 also goes to **Wellington Heath** (Wp.7 49M), introducing possible linear walk alternatives.

From the car park entrance (Wp.1 0M) we go left (W) down a quiet lane with an Elizabethan farmhouse to our right and **The Malverns** behind us. Our way takes us between high hedges behind which orchards can be glimpsed before we reach a T junction (Wp.2 9M) where 'Coddington Vineyard' is signed to the right. Following the sign right, we soon find a stile behind a house on the left, which takes us onto a footpath that passes behind it (SW).

Crossing a field then going along its left edge, we reach a waymarked stile in its corner (Wp.3 12M) and some scrubby vegetation. Next it's up beside a fence into a wood, down the other side to a stile, out into a field and up again to a waymarked stile followed by steps. Another stile takes us into a field with woods on our left; we follow the left hand field edge to another waymarked stile (Wp.4 20M).

From this further field's left edge there are great views to the right over **Bromyard Downs**. Then after going over a stile, we cross a ditch. A steep scramble up between hawthorns brings us to the trig point on the green dome of **Oyster Hill** (Wp.5 27M) where we stop to catch our breath and enjoy views across to the **Welsh Marches** (see photo on next page).

The view from Oyster Hill

Beyond the trig point our way is clear on a wide, grassy path that passes a bench before it's funelled between fences and descends steadily with luxuriant fields to our left and **Berrington Wood** to our right. The obelisk in **Eastnor Park** is to our left on the horizon as we make a good pace along this pleasant path beside the wood.

We cross a stile into a field of long grass with our path mown in front of us. The impressive **Hope End House** together with its walled garden is visible down to our left before the path swings away from the wood (S). We are accompanied by a row of trees to our right before reaching a stile to the left of a wooden barred gate (Wp.6 42M). It's right onto a tarmac track where we meet a lane by **Hope End Farm**.

Right (W) and gently down, again we're alongside **Berrington Wood** which is now up to our right. After passing the village sign for 'Wellington Heath' the lane swings left (SW), **Raycombe Lane** joins us, and we look out for **Swallow Lane Stables** on our left (Wp.7 49M). A footpath by its entrance takes us across two stiles and a paddock to reach a larger field, to continue in the same direction with new housing across the valley to our right. A third stile takes us into a lane where, after another lane joins us, we go gently down with residences to our left as we pass the entrance to **The Farmers Arms**. **Ledbury** is visible ahead of us but quite a long way down; seeming to realise this, the way becomes a path that goes right and left then steeply down between brambles.

Reaching another lane, we ignore the public footpath sign to the left instead following the lane down (W), past a post box in a wall, then around to the left (S) by modern bungalows. Where the lane goes sharp right (Wp.8 61M) we go left towards a large modern house called **Longacres** then in front of it, right through a big metal kissing gate.

After passing in front of the house we go half-left across a field, through an open gate, then along the left edge of the next field to another metal gate in its corner beside a stream. We follow the stream and look for a way over it; a path on the left takes us to a gated bridge (Wp.9 67M).

.. through an apple orchard ..

Now it's right (SSW) on a grassy track through an apple orchard and where the main track goes right, we go straight on into an open space, used as a temporary camp site for fruit pickers during the season.

Beyond it we meet a lane (Wp.10 71M) where we turn left (E) up towards a house surrounded by fruit trees, but before reaching it, veer right onto a stony track then go right again (S) and head towards a cream and black cottage far in the distance. Our way is now between cherry trees grown within a post and wire framework that's covered with netting when the cherries begin to ripen, to protect the crop from birds.

Across the valley is a magnificent 19th century railway viaduct - sadly, in front of it is a ghastly lime green and silver warehouse. Reaching the far side of the orchard we find a metal kissing gate (Wp.11 83M) just to the right which takes us into woods. After another metal kissing gate we meet a track which leads to the left up into **Frith Wood**.

We go right down into a field and follow its top edge to join a larger track (Wp.12 88M SE) where we again go right. After swinging further right (SW) in front of a wood-cladded house, the track climbs steadily up to a road (Wp.13 91M). Here we go straight across (S) past a 'No Through Road' sign into a tiny, residential lane. True to the sign, the tarmac soon ends and we're on a gravel track which descends gently with woods up to our left.

Where the track swings right we carry on behind houses, ignoring a footpath left up into the wood, to arrive at wide concrete steps; a plaque tells us this is the old packhorse road to **Worcester**, and after our lunch stop in **Ledbury** we'll follow its route part of the way back.

After joining a road (Wp.14 99M SW), rather than following a high brick wall around to the left, we nip into the park beyond it.

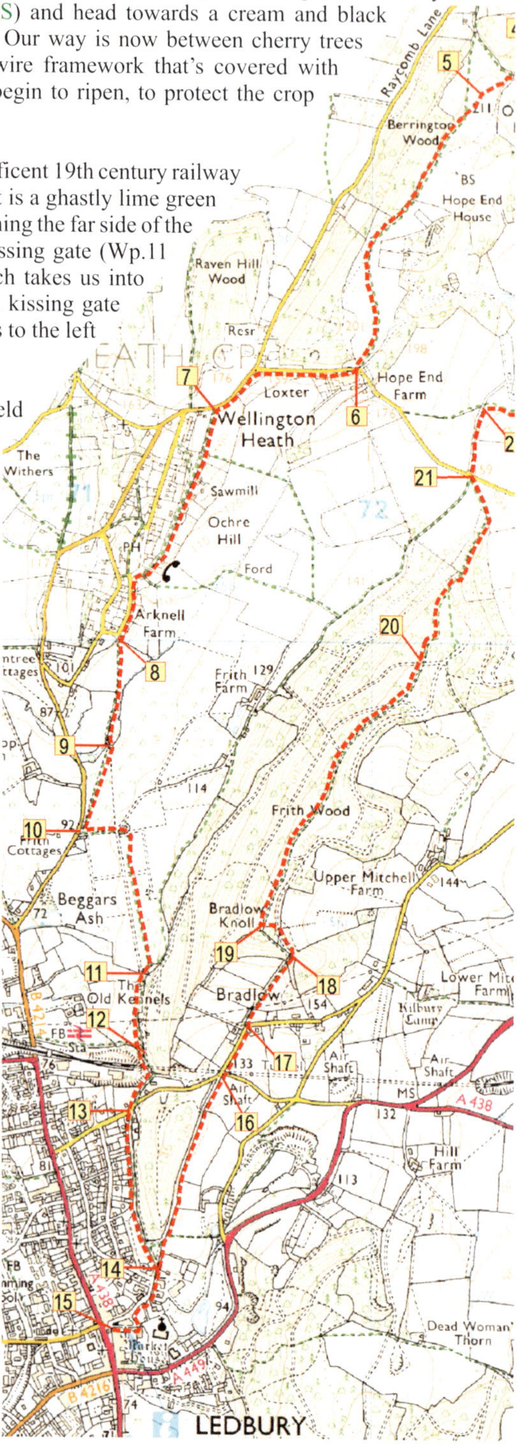

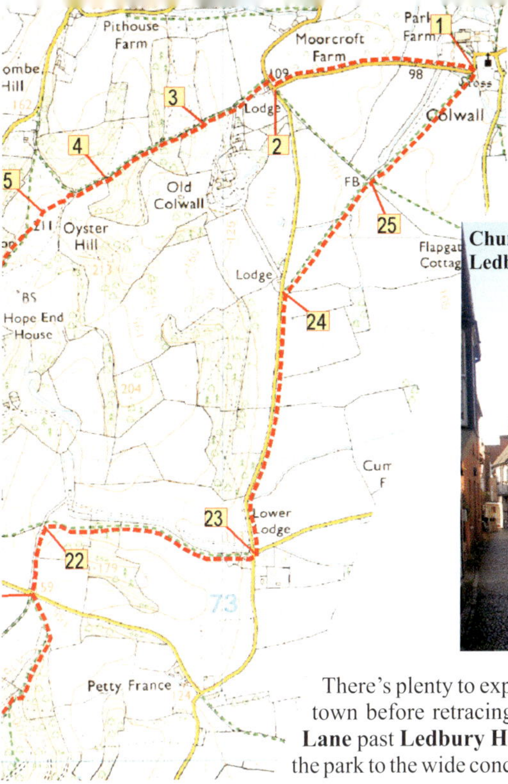

On the park's far side is the delightful, cobbled **Church Lane** which takes us directly to the town centre (Wp.15 102M).

Church Lane, Ledbury

There's plenty to explore in this delightful market town before retracing our steps back up **Church Lane** past **Ledbury Heritage Centre** then through the park to the wide concrete steps (Wp.14 106M).

At a green bench we divert from our inward route into **Ledbury** and go right (NNE) up a sunken lane, making our way along the right hand side of **Dog Hill**. Ignoring a stile to the left and a path up into the wood, we make our way along this wide, woodland path where the prevalence of benches and litter bins demonstrate its popularity. After climbing gently we reach a road (Wp.16 117M) and cross it into a lane opposite, now climbing steadily past sloe berries in the hedgerow.

After the first house on our left (Wp.17 120M) we go left through a wooden barred gate then immediately right (NE) where a sign indicates 'Frith Wood'. Continuing steadily up a green swathe between hedges, we're presented with a choice of gates and take the newer, right hand one to follow the left field edge with our climb growing ever steeper.

At the top of the field, the path continues between brambles and then nettles and after four steps we reach a metal gate (Wp.18 126M). Now we enter **Frith Wood** and the path swings left (NW) before we get to a further flight of steps, this time with a wooden handrail, to reach a junction where a sign confirms that we've reached **Bradley Knowl** (Wp.19 130M). Here we go right with a waymarker and a 'No Horses'sign to follow along a ridge through the woods, ignoring paths to left and right, our way obvious if a little overgrown.

After a path joins us from the right (Wp.20 144M) we cross a wide track and go over a stile before carrying on along the ridge, now with the woodland narrowing so that we can see blue sky beyond it on both sides.

Reaching the end of the ridge, it's steeply down to leave the wood and then diagonally left (NNW) across a field to reach a metal gate into a road (Wp. 21 153M).

We take the track opposite (N), the copse on its left bounded by wooden barred fencing. Where the copse ends we find a stile on the right (Wp.22 156M) to take us alongside another copse (E), skirting a hillock to our right, and going over a stile into a conifer wood. Soon we're over another stile and out of the wood to follow the left hand field edge towards some scattered trees; we keep to the left and reach a stile in the field's corner (Wp.23 165M). Descending between two houses, we go through a metal barred gate to a junction where three lanes meet.

Although 'Colwall' is signed straight on we go left (N) signposted 'Old Colwall' and 'Coddington' along an idyllic, quiet country lane. Though progress here is easy, we need to be careful not to miss the wooden public footpath sign on the right (Wp.24 174M) opposite a metal barred gate and just before a cream cottage on our left. This leads us over a stile and, although there's no obvious path, we set off diagonally left (NE) towards the corner of the field. Nearing it, we notice a gap in the hedge a little to the left and find a plank bridge across a ditch. Continuing in the same direction across the next field, we find a path between stinging nettles in its corner that leads us to a wooden bridge (Wp.25 179M).

Colwall Church

Still in the same direction, we reach a one-off hand crafted gate and now see **Colwall Church** and make directly towards it. Over a stile and up a bank takes us back into its car park (Wp.1 187M). After removing our boots, it's worth taking time to explore the interior of the church.

27 THE DAFFODIL WAY

Though best walked in March or April when the wild daffodils are out, this route is certainly worthwhile at other times as there is much else to enjoy. Starting in **Queen's Wood** near **Kempley Green**, it crosses open farmland before visiting 12th century **Kempley Old Church** with frescoes dating from that period. Then fields and woodland take us around the back of **Dymock** to where its church, (mostly 14th century) has a permanent exhibition devoted to the Dymock Poets. After lunch at the **Beaumont Arms**, the route back takes in **Boyce Court** and **Dymock Wood** - so lots to see, but follow the instructions carefully as, despite having confident 'Public Footpath, The Daffodil Way' signs, the route is not always clear.

Access by car:
From Junction 3 of the M50 head towards **Newent** on the B4221 through **Gorsley** taking the second turning on the left after the post office signposted to 'Kempley' and 'Dymock'. At a T junction, left takes us toward **Kempley** and we park on the left in **Queen's Wood** Forestry Commission car park. OS Grid reference : SO 67793 28435 Nearest postcode : GL18 2BN.

Access by bus:
Nº132 from **Gloucester** to **Ledbury** is the only option; alight at **Dymock** (Wp.39 135M) and the circuit can be walked from there.

Through Queen's Wood

From the car park (Wp.1 0M) we set off left (NNW) along the road, surprised to see **The Malverns** in the distance through a gap in the trees. We walk under an arch of mature trees, then once out of the wood, pass the village sign for 'Kempley' before swinging right and left into the village. A sign reading 'Public Footpath Daffodil Way' points right, our route back.

Shortly after (Wp.2 7M) we follow a similar sign to the left (SW) down the left hand side of a house with a willow tree in its back garden. You'd expect 'The Daffodil Way' to be well-trod but there's not a vestige of a path! Undaunted, we stride out straight forward across the field and then along its right hand edge to find a stile (Wp.3 11M) in its corner. Continuing along the right edge of the next field (W) we reach a bridge across a ditch and then a stile to the right of a farmhouse.

After a similar bridge squeezed between hedges we go left between a farmhouse and stables to a metal gate, then right following a 'Daffodil Way' signpost though a high wooden gate along the back of the stables. This takes us to a further similar bridge (Wp.4 18M) protected by a wooden gate and there we're again presented with no obvious clue to our next direction.

It's straight forward (NW) to the right of a lone oak tree and up to a stile (Wp.5 20M), then down the left side of two fields separated by a stile to a further stile with farm buildings in the field to our left. After two more fields we follow around to the left by trees with more stables to our right and go over a final stile (Wp.6 27M) to reach a road. Here it's right down to a pretty cottage where we turn left, signposted 'Much Marcle' and pass further attractive cottages before swinging left where a steep track leads up to a farm. A rickety wooden barrier, of questionable efficacy, separates us from a deep ditch, perhaps used in snowy conditions to establish the road's edge.

After crossing **Kempley Brook** we climb a stile (Wp.7 34M) to our right and follow the brook's left side (NE) through pasture. A metal kissing gate takes us into more pasture land (NNE); a further new kissing gate, this time beside a five barred gate, takes us into a large field of potatoes (N).

Throughout, we've continued to the left of the brook, just able to see its water between undergrowth along its edge. We find this field is dissected by a ditch and cross it on a bramble and nettle entangled bridge, then continue along its right hand edge.

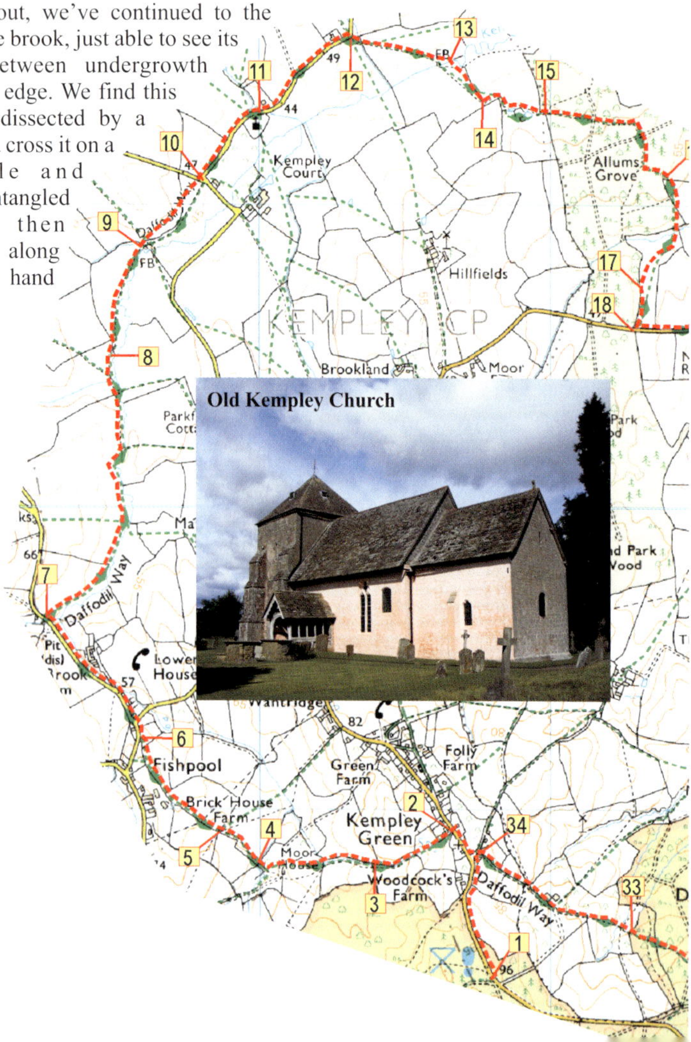

Old Kempley Church

Just before reaching its corner we go right through a gap (Wp.8 48M) to keep along near the brook and make our way, with some difficulty between stinging nettles on the left and a field of maize on the right. Finding a tractor-sized gap in the hedge to our left (Wp.9 54M), we make our way across a grassy field (NE) between electricity poles, then head towards a bungalow.

Getting closer, we spot a metal barred gate to its left and, closer still, a stile hidden in a hedge to the left of it (Wp.10 57M). This takes us to where three lanes meet around an old oak tree. Our way is straight forward signposted 'Dymock' to **Old Kempley Church** (Wp.11 62M), definitely worth looking around, particularly for its brightly coloured frescoes.

After this diversion we continue along the lane until it swings left as we go right over a stile to the left of a metal barred gate (Wp.12 71M) and take the middle of the three footpath options diagonally left through a cereal crop (E).

After a stile hidden in a hedge, we continue towards trees where we cross a bridge (Wp.13 76M) over the now familiar **Kempley Brook** and immediately turn left along the edge of a field. At the field's corner we turn right (SE) and, keeping a sharp eye out, discover a metal kissing gate (Wp.14 79M) in the seriously overgrown hedge to our left.

Next our way is through a field of maize, along its top edge (E) and right to another bridge over a ditch, then left around another field of maize and past a tall, crumbling, brick chimney. Given the chance, we follow the path right through the maize again to meet a wood which we enter via a metal kissing gate (Wp.15 85M). We're now presented with a wide gravel path between tall conifers, such a contrast to where we've just been. After crossing a track, the gravel underfoot disappears and the path narrows; then we swing right (SE), cross another track and reach a metal kissing gate (Wp.16 91M) that takes us out of the wood to follow its edge.

Another kissing gate takes us back into the wood, continuing in the same direction but now just inside it, gently down then swinging right. Yet another metal kissing gate takes us to a couple of bridges and out into a field populated with virulent thistles. We go diagonally right (SW), cutting across the field's corner to meet the wood again at a stile (Wp.17 100M) where we follow its edge (S) to meet a road (Wp.18 103M) and turn left (E).

First it's gently up between hedges then past **New Rock**, a classic timber-framed Elizabethan farmhouse then, shortly after a post box hidden in the hedge, we turn left (N) off the road (Wp.19 110M), down the right hand side of a field by a bungalow. At the bottom of the field we go through a wooden kissing gate into an orchard. Keeping parallel to its right hand boundary, we follow it around to the right (NE) until we come to a metal gate (Wp.20 115M). This takes us out of the orchard where we head towards the left of a barn (N), then swing slowly right (ENE) until we're beside the left hand field edge, following it until we meet a gravel farm track (Wp.21 116M).

The track leads to a road (Wp.22 122M) where we turn right (SE) and soon see signs for 'Dymock' but before entering the village we cross the road and turn left (ENE) down a further track to 'Maypole Farm'. Almost immediately it's right (ESE) over a stile (Wp.23 124M) and across to the far corner of the field, ignoring the inviting wooden bridge - that's not our way.

In the far corner there's another bridge, straight after which we go left (SE) beside a maize field, then right (S) through the maize towards **Dymock Church**. A metal kissing gate (Wp.24 131M) takes us into its churchyard and we go around the right of the church and through its lychgate to find the **Beauchamp Arms** conveniently next door (Wp.25 135M).

After our thoroughly deserved stop, we locate a stile opposite the pub and go down the right hand side of a field (S), then in its corner negotiate a tangle of shrubbery out into a field of thistles. After a metal kissing gate (Wp.26 140M) we go left and around a large field with the main house of **Boyce Court** prominent on the horizon to our right. In the field's far corner there's another metal kissing gate, after which we continue down the left of the next field until we spot a bridge (Wp.27 150M) which takes us onto a path between a stream and a ditch through overgrown woodland. The path ends with steps taking us up to a further metal kissing gate where we meet a track (Wp.28 153M).

We go right over an old brick bridge, then immediately left between brick pillars into the estate of **Boyce Court**. The track, with grass in its middle, leads us right and left past a pond populated by varied wild fowl. At a cattle grid, we leave the estate's grounds.

A farm track (SW) takes us towards **Timber Hill Farm** where after another cattle grid (Wp.29 164M) we swing right in front of the farmhouse. After passing it we go left through a metal kissing gate (Wp.30 166M) and along the left of yet another field of maize (S). First we hear the sound of the motorway, then see the cars rushing by ahead of us while in contrast ducks quietly get on with their lives in a pond below. Swinging to the right around the edge of the field (SW) with the M50 on an embankment above us, we make our way through a metal kissing gate, over a track that itself goes under the motorway and through two further metal gates up to meet a road (Wp.31 175M).

.. wild daffodils ..

Our way is left along it, parallel to the motorway, where wild daffodils border the woodland.

The noise seems so out of place that on meeting a road it's pleasant to turn right (NW) away from it through **Dymock Wood**.

Dymock Wood

Before long there's a track to the left (Wp.32 180M W) which quickly becomes a delightful woodland path. Signs inform us that we're on the 'Three Choirs Way' which we encountered miles away on Walk 13 Madresfield Court, it would be interesting to know how it got from there to here - perhaps we should walk it!

Carrying on, we keep to the main right hand spur at a fork to cross a track before leaving the wood at a wooden kissing gate (Wp.33 186M). Unaccountably, the substantial path that we've been following now disappears but we go straight on (WNW), crossing a ditch under a willow tree before making our way up to a metal kissing gate. Then it's left of a corrugated iron barn where, in the far right hand corner, we find a further kissing gate hidden in a dip. Continuing up the right hand field edge, we pass through a wooden kissing gate and between two closely clipped hedges before arriving at the 'Daffodil Way' sign we noticed soon after our start (Wp.34 197M). There we go left along the lane (S), back through **Queen's Wood** to the car park (Wp.1 202M) - not the easiest walk in this book, but maybe all the more satisfying for that.

28 AROUND HAUGH WOOD

In a little-known area alongside the **River Wye** south east of **Hereford**, this walk takes part of the **Mordiford Loop Walk** and extends it down the east side of the extensive **Haugh Wood** to the village of **Fownhope**, then goes through much wilder woodland over **Cherry Hill** to **Mordiford** where it rejoins the loop walk to return. Be aware that although the greatest height achieved is only 175 metres total ascent/descent is 360 metres as there are four significant climbs.

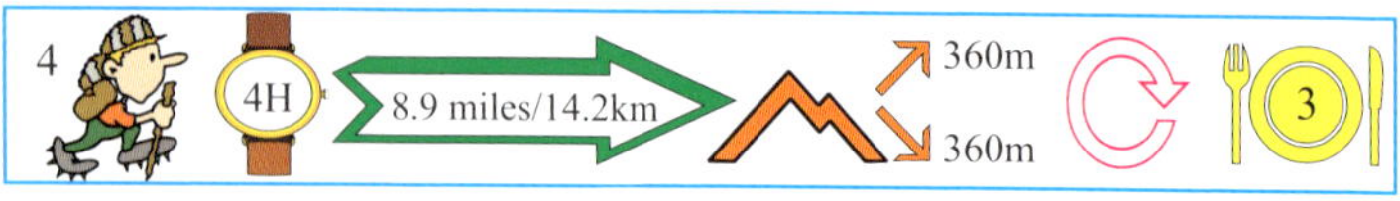

Access by car:
From junction 2 of the M50, follow the A417 towards **Ledbury** and follow the ring road to the A438 signposted 'Hereford'. After crossing the A417 and passing through **Stoke Edith** take a tiny lane on the left to **Upper Dormington**. Don't be put off by the grass in the middle; it is a through road. After passing through **Prior's Frome** fork left signposted 'Woolhope' and 'Checkley' to reach **Swarndon Quarry Picnic Place** on the right. OS Grid reference : SO 57788 38537 Postcode : HR1 4EJ.

Access by bus:
Getting to the start by bus is a non-starter. However, bus N°453 runs from **Hereford** to **Fownhope** (Wp.23 133M), our lunch break, and also stops at **Mordiford** (Wp.31 205M).

Viewpoint above Swarndon Quarry Picnic Place

Before setting off we climb steps from the car park to the signed viewpoint to soak in the panoramic view west. Then from **Swarndon Quarry Picnic Place** (Wp.1 0M) we go steadily up the lane to the right (ESE), swinging further right before reaching a stony track on the left (Wp.2 5M) signed 'Mordiford Loop Walk'.

The track goes almost immediately right but we carry straight on, steadily up a path between cow parsley through woodland, bare rock beneath us in places.

After ignoring a path on the left we come to a fork (Wp.3 11M) and follow the main, well-trodden path right (E) to skirt **Backbury Hill**. We ignore a footpath on our right before starting gently down and swinging to the left (NE). It's steadily down by wooden fencing until we join a track (Wp.4 21M). At a T junction, with conifers to our left, we turn right into a lane (S). Almost immediately, opposite a cottage (Wp.5 25M), we go through a metal gate in the hedge on the left (SE) into a 'buttercups and daisies' field with glorious views ahead.

After the first field we drop steeply down a bank to the next one, then it's gently down across a couple more fields until we pass a new plantation of trees and come to a black timbered house that's being restored and cross a stile by a wooden barred gate to a lane (Wp.6 32M). Turning left ,we keep straight on where our **Mordiford Loop Walk** companion goes right, but immediately after the lane turns left (Wp.7 36M) we go right (ESE) though a black painted gate beside a black and white timbered cottage. We head up the right hand side of their garden to find a wooden gate into an orchard; going left between the trees, we reach a little wooden footbridge and a gate (Wp.8 39M) that takes us into another orchard.

Following the right hand hedge, we reach a stile (Wp.9 42M) and go left (E) onto a path to reach another stile to the right of a metal barred gate. We're into a nondescript area of cow parsley, stinging nettles, decaying trees and hawthorns but this soon leads to a lane (Wp.10 46M) where we go right (SW) over a cattle grid between an avenue of coppiced hazels towards two modern houses. Passing through a wooden gate to the left of the second one, we continue in the same direction over a stile to the left of a rusty gate and to an overgrown orchard which feels ethereally peaceful.

On its far side a larger footbridge (Wp.11 51M) takes us across **Pentaloe Brook** into a flower-bedecked meadow with no sign that any walker has been here before! Following the right hand edge of the field towards woodland we find a stile half way up (Wp.12 55M) and cross it; unaccountably there now is a defined path which takes us gently up a field with woodland left and right. At the top of this field we go a little left (SSW) with another path even further left. Now it's steadily up with dense woods on our left until we reach a stile to the right of a new metal barred gate which takes us into **Haugh Wood** (Wp.13 63M).

There's a number of ways through this large Forestry Commission managed area; ours is along a major track pretty much in the same direction, ignoring alternatives to left and right. The easily-walked track meanders through these beautiful, mature woods, at one point crossing a ravine until, eventually, we meet a road (Wp.14 81M).

Turning right (W) we head towards a Forestry Commission sign, then go left beside a pole barrier (Wp.15 83M SW) past freshly hewn logs. Where the main track swings right we go straight on, descending gently at first, then steadily past elegant, tall beech trees. At the bottom, just after the track swings left (Wp.16 90M), we turn right to continue in the same direction, now close to the edge of the wood. Again the way meanders, this time with stunning views along the valley to our left until the track turns right (Wp.17 101M) and we go left (S), steeply down a path that becomes rocky before reaching another pole barrier and another track (Wp.18 104M).

We go left (SE) down to a road (Wp.19 106M) and left again (E), then almost immediately right opposite a cream and black cottage, across a stile and through a field of long grass (S). After crossing a stream via a wooden footbridge we climb gently between wheat. At the top it's over one stile (Wp.20 113M) then almost immediately over another to go left (SSE), steadily up between hedge and wood.

We cross the **Wye Valley Walk** and go down a tarmac track to the right with grass in its middle (SSW) to join a lane by a telephone box (Wp.21 119M). This delightful lane sweeps right (W) then has wonderful views forward, at one point with an unhindered vista of **Hay Bluff**.

After reaching modern residential developments on the outskirts of **Fownhope** we leave the road where it swings left (Wp.22 130M) to go to the right of two garages along a tarmac path, by the front of some houses and down steps past **Fownhope New Memorial Hall** to reach the main road (Wp.23 133M) opposite the **New Inn** with its 'Ramblers Welcome' sign.

Turning left (NW) on leaving the pub after that oh so welcome stop, we pass the **Green Man** and the fire station before, on the opposite side of the road, crossing a metal bridge where pedestrians are separated from vehicles

At the next corner by a lane signed 'Woolhope' (Wp.24 136M), we find a village pump in an attractive stone enclosure.

The village pump, Fownhope

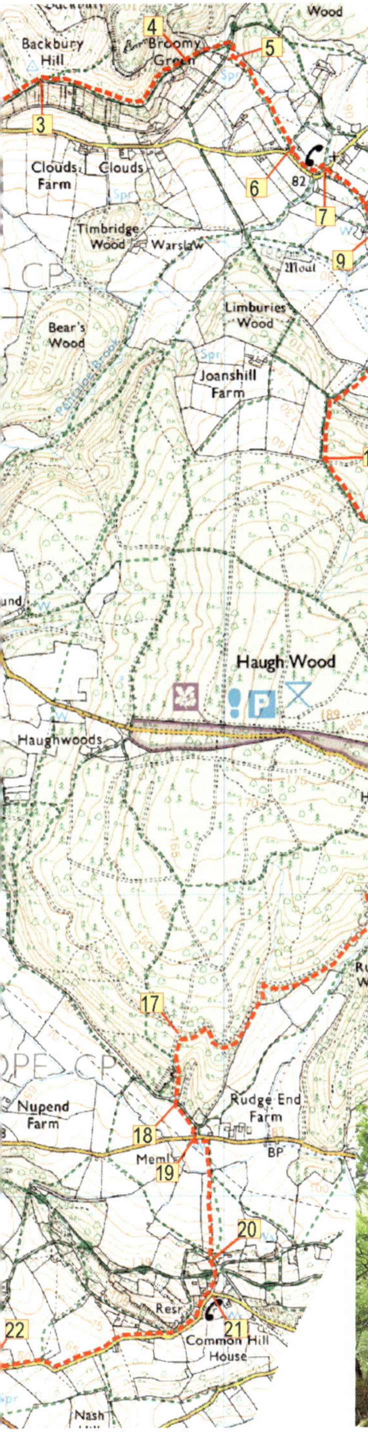

We gently ascend the lane right (NNE) past modern bungalows. Taking an inauspicious path left, almost hidden by stinging nettles (Wp.25 138M), we climb shallow steps (WNW), seemingly in the wrong direction, to the back of houses, then swing right (N) and start steadily climbing through woods - now we're happier!

There are several alternatives but we keep to the main path, swinging left (NNW) on a long, steady climb up a ridge, steep down on either side, to reach earthworks, the remains of a fort on the top of **Cherry Hill**. There are no views as we are deep in woodland and there's no summit as such but our breathlessness indicates that it's a worthy achievement just the same. We start dropping gently through a gap in the earthworks, then it's steadily up again with the land continuing to drop away steeply to the right.

Given the chance, we fork right (Wp.26 160M) to go first very steeply down then, after crossing a track steeply up and a little to the right (N). Swinging back left (NW) we're now on another ridge, passing first between brambles amid conifers

.. a ridge through ancient woodland ..

then through ancient woodland where we begin descending gently.

Forking right off the ridge (Wp.27 173M) we realize it's only to avoid the tangle of roots that have been making progress tricky so we get back on it when the going becomes easier and can now see a green field beyond the wood to our right. Dropping down steeply again, we come to a sunken lane crossing our path (Wp.28 179M) where we go right then almost immediately left (N) onto a path that follows the edge of **West Wood** and shortly joins a forest track. We stay on this for a good while, enjoying the easier walking.

Passing a bench, amused by its position; once there was obviously a view from it, long since obscured by tangled growth.

Eventually the track swings long left (WNW) and we find ourselves between sweet chestnuts as we go gently down but, aware that we are going back on ourselves, turn acute right given the chance (Wp.29 186M) to follow another track (NNE) on the flat where we get a glimpse of the **River Wye** between a gap in the trees.

River Wye

To the right of a pole barrier we're into a car park (Wp.30 201M) and turn right along the main road to **Mordiford**. Entering the village, we cross the road to the safety of the pavement before crossing **Pentaloe Brook** again. As the main road goes left by **The Moon Inn** (Wp.31 205M) we go right (E), along a lane with neat black railings enclosing a graveyard to our left and a brook babbling to our right.

A track on the left (Wp.32 208M) is signposted with our former companion's name of 'Mordiford Loop Walk' and we now follow it back almost to the start. Our way is up behind houses (ENE) rather than along the track even further to the left. Just before reaching a gate (Wp.33 211M) we find a footpath on the left where cow parsley attempts to restrict our progress, first up steps and then steadily up through woodland (NE).

At a stile (Wp.34 217M) we leave the wood and go slightly right (ENE) to follow the edge of a field, now gently upwards past an oak tree with a metal ladder reaching up into its lower boughs. Going between gateposts into the next field, we follow its left edge by a coppice, steadily turning to the left (N). 'Circular Walk' signs lead us over a stile with **Backbury Hill** prominent straight in front of us. Now on a grassy track, it's steadily down between more gateposts (Wp.35 232M) to a stile to the right of a metal barred gate. After another stile is the welcome sight of the sign (Wp.36 236M) indicating that 'Swarndon Quarry' is only 150 yards to the left. Following its pointing finger, (W) we go down steeply to a track then right to reach a lane and find the car park to our left (Wp.1 239M).

29 FOWNHOPE AND CAPLER CAMP

This varied walk follows the **Wye Valley Way** for most of the morning, passing the iron age fort of **Capler Camp** and going through **Lea and Paget's Nature Reserve** before leaving the long distance footpath to drop down into **Fownhope** for a lunch stop. We return alongside the meandering **River Wye**, finishing with a brief climb back to the start.

Walks 28 and 29 can be combined to form a figure of eight route with **The Moon** at **Mordiford** as the lunch stop. Start as this walk but at **The New Inn** in **Fownhope**, change to Walk 28, following it from Wp.23, past its start to Wp.21 then change back to Walk 29 to finish along beside the river.

Access by car:
From junction 4 at the end of the M50 take the A449 towards **Ledbury** then turn left onto the B4224 signposted 'Fownhope' and 'Hereford'. After 3.7 miles (5.9 km) we turn left into a narrow lane signposted 'Brockhampton' and after a crossroads and a straggle of houses turn right into a nondescript picnic site named **Brinkley Hill**. OS Grid reference : SO 58437 31282 Postcode : HR1 4SL

Access by bus:
The only possibility is to take bus N°453 which runs from **Hereford** to **Fownhope** (our lunch stop at Wp.24) and to walk the circuit from there.

We start out from the uninspiring picnic site (Wp.1 0M) which gives no hint that the stunningly beautiful **River Wye** is so close. It's back along the lane we've arrived along to begin (NE), passing the village sign for 'Brockhampton' and some scattered cottages until the **Wye Valley Walk** diagonally crosses our route (Wp.2 8M) and we follow this well-known long distance footpath to the left, almost to **Fownhope** so you might expect route finding to be a doddle, but this is not always so! Our way is a track, initially between hedges then with a conifer wood to our left.

.. hand crafted wooden benches ..

After the last wayward cottage, the trees either side draw together and it's gently upwards then briefly steeply upwards before we meet a road (Wp.3 16M) and turn left (NNW). Here, another picnic site, infinitely superior to the one we've come from, has an information board, hand crafted wooden benches and a fabulous view through trees down to the **River Wye**.

Just as the road begins to drop downward (Wp.4 19M) we take a right (NNW),

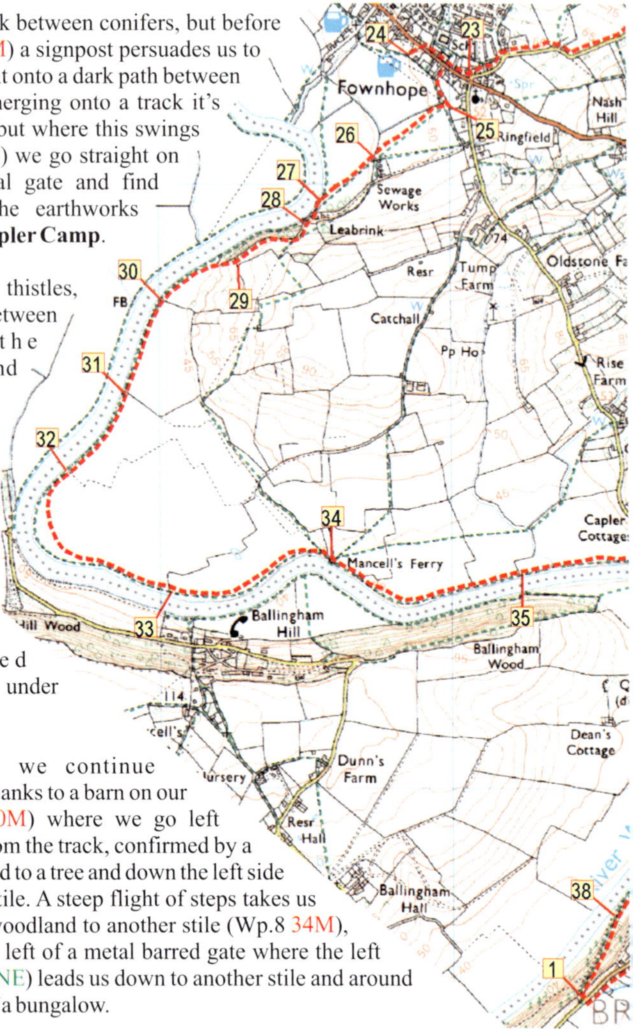

following a track between conifers, but before long (Wp.5 24M) a signpost persuades us to dive further right onto a dark path between dense trees. Emerging onto a track it's right again (E) but where this swings left (Wp.6 26M) we go straight on through a metal gate and find ourselves in the earthworks surrounding **Capler Camp**.

Surrounded by thistles, we go left up between a gap in the earthworks and find a large enclosed field. It's easy to imagine this place overflowing with local inhabitants and their livestock congregated together when under attack.

Withdrawing, we continue between earth banks to a barn on our right (Wp.7 30M) where we go left (ENE) away from the track, confirmed by a waymark pinned to a tree and down the left side of a field to a stile. A steep flight of steps takes us down though woodland to another stile (Wp.8 34M), this time to the left of a metal barred gate where the left side of a field (NE) leads us down to another stile and around the right side of a bungalow.

Continuing down the left side of the next field. we go between recently planted trees before emerging into the car park of a farm shop (Wp.9 39M). Left and right take us onto a substantial gravel track which leads to a relatively busy road (Wp.10 41M). We turn left (NW), cross the road and start up a hill; the way's quite narrow so it's a relief to turn right onto a stony track. Almost immediately we go right over a stile (Wp.11 43M NE) and make our way through a field of clover towards another stile, which we can just make out on the far side.

After clambering over it (Wp.12 46M) we go around the field we're confronted with, first right, then down left and left again until we reach a concrete bridge (Wp.13 49M) on our right. This takes us across a brook and we follow the left hand edge of the field (N), rather than the more obvious path straight on up the hillock ahead.

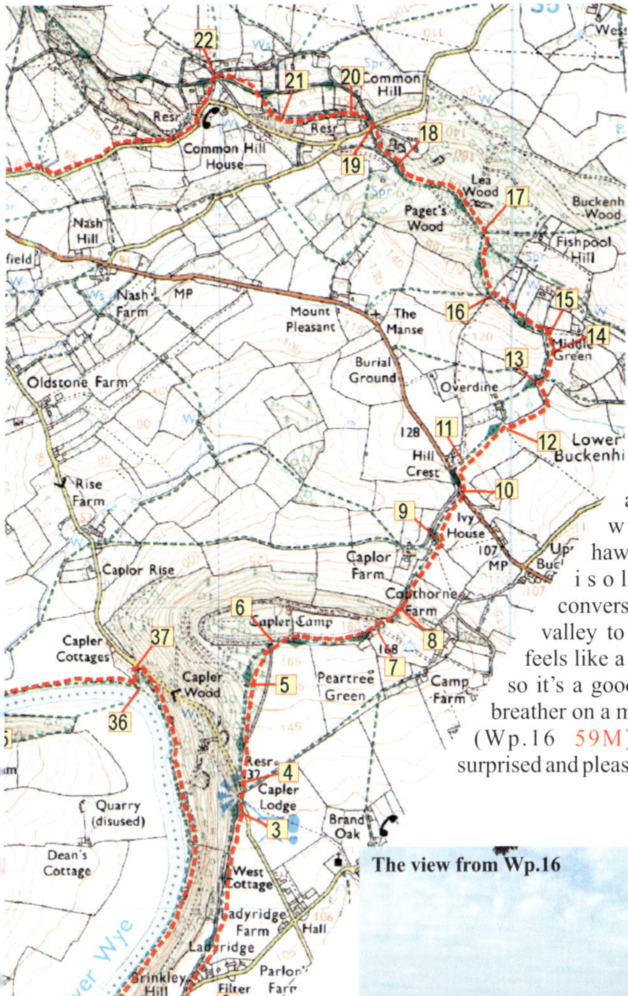

At another stile (Wp.14 51M) we follow a signpost left then, at the corner of the field, go right up towards an oak tree and find a stile hiding behind it (Wp.15 53M).

It's up the left hand side of the next field as well (NW), this time through an avenue of wizened hawthorns with an isolated barn conversion down in the valley to our right. That feels like a lot of climbing, so it's a good idea to take a breather on a metal park bench (Wp.16 59M) that we're surprised and pleased, to find here.

The view from Wp.16

Setting off again, we go over a stile into a wood, where an information board proclaims **Lea and Paget's Nature Reserve**, and follow a good path through woods, going straight on where five paths meet (Wp.17 62M) then gently down. A stile to the right of a wooden barred gate (Wp.18 68M) takes us out of the wood by a paddock and where the path divides we fork right to go steadily upward and through a couple of gates to meet a lane (Wp.19 71M).

Along the ridge

Crossing it, we go up the right hand side of **Common Hill Farm** and left (W) around its perimeter, then through a wooden gate on the right (Wp.20 73M) and down a couple of steps, continuing in the same direction with the land dropping steeply away to our right.

After another wooden gate we're in woodland which straddles **Common Hill** until we come to a wooden kissing gate (Wp.21 77M) which takes us right (NW) and steeply down across a field.

Another gate takes us onto a path, now steadily downwards to a choice of ways (Wp.22 81M); here we leave the **Wye Valley Walk** and select the steepest option to the left, a tarmac track with grass in its centre.

This takes us further down (SW) past an ancient green pump housed in what looks like a bus shelter to join a quiet lane that swings gently to the right (WSW) on its way down to **Fownhope**.

Reaching a crossroads (Wp.23 94M) with the parish church on our left we go right (NW) to find our lunch stop, **The New Inn**, set back from the road on the left (Wp.24 98M).

After this welcome stop we go back along the road (SE) until we spot a wooden public footpath sign that leads us right (SW) between high brick walls then left (SE) behind houses into a recreation ground (Wp.25 103M). There it's right again (SW), across a football pitch and in front of a pavilion, making for the right hand end of a tall hedge (Wp.26 108M).

River Wye at Fownhope

Here we find a gap into a field and following its left hand edge, reach the **River Wye** (Wp.27 112M) where a bench is splendidly situated to enjoy the view. To the left of it we go through a gate into the garden of an attractive house, then scamper across their terrace as there's a sense of intruding even though it's a public right of way.

Then it's steep up through woodland where, at a choice of ways (Wp.28 114M) we go right, over a stile, and even more steeply up a bank.

Out of the wood, we follow the field edge around to the right; buzzards may be spotted wheeling overhead here; then, a little to the left, we go through an open gate (Wp.29 119M). The view is to die for as we drop steeply down around the edge of woodland to meet the river again.

Our way beside the tranquil waters is now very relaxing. We go over first one stile (Wp.30 125M), then another (Wp.31 130M) under a willow tree. After a stile to the right of a metal barred gate (Wp.32 134M), we can see the river ahead circling to the left and the path moves to the left , running beside a field.

Now closer to the river again (ESE) it's shallower and therefore running faster - you may meet a horde of Canada geese before coming to a further stile (Wp.33 145M). The main path goes left but we keep on beside the river; what superb views the houses up to the right on the other side of the river must have.

Another pair of stiles (Wp.34 155M) take us into and out of the garden of an isolated cottage and further on we stare at three, seemingly unoccupied, teepees on the opposite bank and wonder if this is an example of glamping. At a stile under another willow (Wp.35 166M E) we can see woods reaching up in front of us and, after a bridge over a minor tributary, we climb over the obligatory stile into their shelter (Wp.36 173M). It's sharp left (NNW) and steep up by a fence, but shortly we reach a track (Wp.37 176M) where we turn right (SE) grateful to be on the flat again.

Bizarrely, there may be the sounds of cars, obviously on a road nearby, though they aren't visible. We start descending, still in woodland, but now slowly swinging right (S) on this stony track to meet the river yet again. Now we're walking on what looks like a wide strip of green carpet that separates the woodland from the river, then for a time the way becomes a track, and later it's back to green carpet (SW).

We see the spire of the church at **Ballingham** to the right, poking above the horizon which means it's time to keep a watchful eye out for a track going up to the left though woods (Wp.38 194M). This takes us steadily upwards (SSW), then ever steeper until, quite surprisingly, we pop out into our originating **Brinkley Hill** car park (Wp.1 199M). What a splendid day out!

30 MAY HILL

If you stand on the top of **Chase End Hill** at the southern end of the **Malvern Hills** and look south, a bump with what looks like a scruffy head of hair can be seen in the distance; this conspicuous landmark is **May Hill**. The walk not only encompasses **May Hill** itself, the village of **Clifford's Mesne**, **Newent Woods** and **Huntley Ponds**, but also includes the chance to visit **The Glasshouse** and the **Yew Tree Inn**, both highly recommended eateries.

Access by car:
From junction 4 of the M50, which is at the end of the motorway, carry on to the next roundabout then turn left onto the A40 heading back towards **Gloucester**. After 7.8 miles (12.5 km) and a turning on the right to **Longhope**, turn left onto a minor road signposted 'May Hill' and 'Cliffords Mesne' and keep on it until reaching **The Glasshouse** on the right. In addition to the pub car park, there is another place to park just beyond it. OS Grid reference : SO 70967 21359 Nearest postcode : GL17 0NW

Access by bus:
The best suggestion is to take bus N°33 that trundles from **Gloucester** to **Ross on Wye** along the A40, get off at **Dursley Cross**, make your way up to (Wp.5) at the foot of **May Hill** and complete the circuit from there.

The Topiary House

Opposite **The Glasshouse** (Wp.1 0M) it's worth taking a look at the amazing topiary house before going right (NW) along a lane signposted 'Clifford's Mesne'. After only a minute there's a lane on our right signposted 'Newent' and opposite it a stile by a wide metal barred gate with a 'Wysis Way' public footpath sign (Wp.2 1M) which we take.

This leads us steadily up a track through woodland (WSW) and right at a fork, following a waymark before the track degenerates into a path and becomes steeper. Many varieties of toadstools thrive here amid the mix of coniferous and deciduous trees, as the path flattens but then it climbs again before reaching a crossroads (Wp.3 20M).

We turn left (S) through a new metal kissing gate to the right of a rusty old metal gate and almost immediately cross a larger track to follow a signpost to 'May Hill' (WSW). This delightful tree-lined path takes us steadily upwards with foliage meeting overhead. We pass between concrete posts before swinging right onto a larger path (Wp.4 24M WNW). After crossing another track we go around a metal barrier (Wp.5 26M) and soon the way underfoot is reinforced with grey shale, an indication of the popularity of this route.

At a further metal gate (Wp.6 29M) we pass into the auspices of the National Trust with a beech wood on our right and open grassland progressively opening up (NW).

At a fork of two wide grassy paths we keep to the right, heading towards the group of conifers on the summit of **May Hill** which so define it. Getting closer, with gorse and bracken on either side of us, we spot a trig point to our left just in front of the trees but pass to the right of them.

On top of May Hill

Looking west from May hill - and toadstool

There are great views west and some magnificent toadstools as we continue in the same direction keeping to the right of a large clump of gorse bushes then begin to descend. At a wooden gate to the right of a metal barred one (Wp.7 45M) our way is a little to the right (NE) with alternative paths to both sides, back in attractive woodland and now going steadily down.

A path crosses us (Wp.8 52M) before we join a lane (Wp.9 55M) continuing in the same direction, still downhill, still through woodland, and over an unusual diamond-patterned cattle grid before reaching the **Yew Tree Inn** (Wp.10 61M). This recommended pub, and not just by us according to the plaudits on display, is the first building we reach on the outskirts of **Cliffords Mesne**; straight after it we come to a T junction and turn left (NW). First we follow the lane around to the right then take the rightmost option, a residential road signposted to 'Newent' (NE), which gently bears left (N).

After **Pear Tree Cottage** we turn right (Wp.11 66M ENE) down an unpaved track signed as a 'Restricted Byeway' then at a T junction turn left onto a tarmacked track passing **Honeysuckle Cottage**, a large home to be described as a cottage, before reaching a road (Wp.12 70M). Here we turn right (E) passing **Lower Farmhouse** then a fairy tale cottage and an entry into **Huntley Estate** on our right.

.. fairytale woodsman's cottage ..

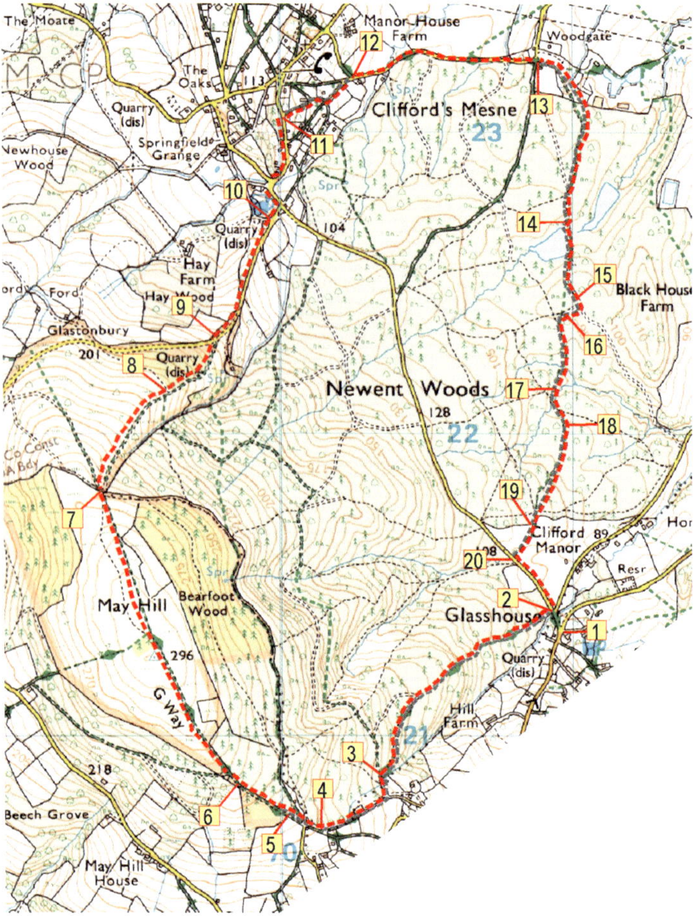

Continuing along the road with woods to our right and open farmland to our left, we carry on until the road turns left (Wp.13 76M). Here it's straight on, not taking the signed public footpath but going between brick pillars, the entrance to **Woodgate Farm**.

Huntley Ponds

Very soon we go right (SE), diving into woods past a wooden barrier. Again it's beautiful woodland and, although the path is overgrown, the way is still obvious as it slowly swings further right (S). After a track joins us from the left, we come to an open space surrounded by piles of logs and shortly afterwards reach serene **Huntley Ponds** (Wp.14

86M). Ignoring paths left and right we go straight on, alongside one of the ponds, to reach a small car park on its far side.

We now follow the track motorists use to access this beauty spot but, given the chance (Wp.15 91M), turn right (W) onto a smaller track then left on to a footpath (Wp.16 92M S). There is a waymark here but it's cunningly placed behind a tree so it's tricky to spot! Next we continue through these delightful woods, ignoring a larger path with hoof prints to the right (Wp.17 97M) but later going right slightly uphill (Wp.18 98M SW).

After joining another logging track we cross a grassy way and come to a stile (Wp.19 104M) which takes us out of the wood and through a field of maize, to another stile and a lane (Wp.20 107M). Left here (SE) takes us back to where we first entered woodland (Wp.2 110M) and straight on back to **The Glasshouse** (Wp.1 111M).

WAYPOINT LISTS

See the notes on 'Using GPS in the Malverns' on page 15.

1

BREDON HILL FROM WESTMANCOTE

Wp	Zn	North	East
1	SO	92798	37496
2	SO	92734	37297
3	SO	93338	37528
4	SO	93808	37589
5	SO	94323	38048
6	SO	94582	38316
7	SO	94539	39218
8	SO	94824	39709
9	SO	95319	39912
10	SO	95672	40178
11	SO	96261	40306
12	SO	96721	40252
13	SO	96821	40125
14	SO	96430	39778
15	SO	96059	38914
16	SO	95822	38519
17	SO	95815	38072
18	SO	95990	37833
19	SO	95806	37416
20	SO	95728	37329
21	SO	95543	37221
22	SO	94854	36891
23	SO	94564	36733
24	SO	94575	37199
25	SO	94522	36933
26	SO	93796	36999
27	SO	93619	37239

2

OVERBURY

Wp	Zn	North	East
1	SO	95740	37449
2	SO	96016	37807
3	SO	96004	38642
5	SO	96408	39778
6	SO	96815	40118
7	SO	97382	39531
8	SO	97889	39300
9	SO	8569	38447
10	SO	98666	38346
11	SO	99524	37934
12	SO	99636	37715
13	SO	99736	37801
14	SO	99028	37330
15	SO	98842	37218
16	SO	98373	37308
17	SO	98068	37161
18	SO	97877	37152
19	SO	96994	37126
20	SO	96561	37210
21	SO	96470	37226
22	SO	96165	37346
23	SO	95880	37558

3

ELMLEY CASTLE

Wp	Zn	North	East
1	SO	98245	41191
2	SO	98027	41233
3	SO	97899	41245
4	SO	97428	40852
5	SO	97253	40770
6	SO	97089	40522
7	SO	96803	40367
8	SO	96813	40124
9	SO	97398	39540
10	SO	97576	39628
11	SO	97894	39764
12	SO	98051	39951
13	SO	98126	39902
14	SO	98178	39762
15	SO	98329	39610
17	SO	98504	39441
18	SO	99003	38809
19	SO	99052	38460
20	SO	99126	38353
21	SO	99722	38223
22	SO	99744	37815
23	SO	99768	38542
24	SO	99680	38890
25	SO	99598	39085
26	SO	99561	39224
27	SO	99455	39285
28	SO	99378	39346
29	SO	99400	39595
30	SO	99375	39687
31	SO	99280	39876
32	SO	99018	39867
33	SO	98836	40095
34	SO	98796	40303
35	SO	98634	40470
36	SO	98561	40573
37	SO	98317	40907

4

WOOLLAS HALL

Wp	Zn	North	East
1	SO	94583	40939
2	SO	94792	40626
3	SO	95058	40607
4	SO	95150	40487
5	SO	95235	40077
6	SO	95222	39849
7	SO	95255	39851
8	SO	95323	39912
9	SO	95574	40088
10	SO	95669	40180
11	SO	94839	39708
12	SO	94790	39493
13	SO	94541	39217
14	SO	94544	39142
15	SO	94253	39355
16	SO	94019	39127
17	SO	93877	39031
18	SO	93575	38898
19	SO	93440	38896
20	SO	93325	38978
21	SO	93334	39067
22	SO	93753	39815
23	SO	94132	40334
24	SO	94305	40376

5

ECKINGTON BRIDGE

Wp	Zn	North	East
1	SO	92241	42252
2	SO	92237	42356
3	SO	92893	42495
4	SO	93077	42455
5	SO	93107	42610
6	SO	93332	42593
7	SO	93497	42508
8	SO	94091	41971
9	SO	94095	41697
10	SO	94639	41752
11	SO	94888	41896
12	SO	95113	41923
13	SO	95355	42045
14	SO	95372	41824
15	SO	95468	41468
16	SO	95701	41105
17	SO	94896	40761
18	SO	94787	40630
19	SO	94533	41157
20	SO	94312	41085
21	SO	93868	41331
22	SO	92928	41484
23	SO	92332	41314
24	SO	92251	41265
25	SO	92041	41138
26	SO	91571	40463
27	SO	91734	42458

6

PERSHORE BRIDGE AND TIDDESLEY WOOD

Wp	Zn	North	East
1	SO	95246	45081
2	SO	95197	45120
3	SO	94561	44851
4	SO	93716	44927
5	SO	93962	45274
6	SO	93734	45217
7	SO	93362	45388
8	SO	93130	45399

Wp	Zn	North	East
9	SO	92789	45342
10	SO	92668	45326
11	SO	92643	46052
12	SO	92953	45954
13	SO	93528	45721
14	SO	93671	46119
15	SO	94273	45961
16	SO	94726	45848
17	SO	94770	45812
18	SO	94935	45860
19	SO	94852	45710
20	SO	94835	45508
21	SO	95041	45339

7

THE SEVERN AND THE AVON

Wp	Zn	North	East
1	SO	88685	37743
2	SO	88742	37598
3	SO	88589	37507
4	SO	88377	37647
5	SO	88235	37619
6	SO	88077	37588
7	SO	87927	37694
8	SO	87851	37715
9	SO	87721	37704
10	SO	87568	37766
11	SO	87268	37770
12	SO	86840	37945
13	SO	86588	37779
14	SO	86389	37643
15	SO	86290	37606
16	SO	86753	36941
17	SO	86862	36368
18	SO	87250	35659
19	SO	87851	34834
20	SO	88421	34396
21	SO	88643	34219
22	SO	88715	34137
23	SO	88906	33787
24	SO	89027	33760
25	SO	89361	33244
26	SO	89247	33002
27	SO	89197	32726
28	SO	89239	32648
29	SO	89002	32485
30	SO	89289	33361
31	SO	89486	33737
32	SO	89729	34291
33	SO	89857	34880
34	SO	90161	35449
35	SO	90382	36264
36	SO	90447	36510
37	SO	90386	36553
38	SO	90351	36753
39	SO	90447	37105
40	SO	90198	37146
41	SO	89943	37204
42	SO	89846	37253
43	SO	89715	37142
44	SO	89276	37106
45	SO	89000	37319

8

ODDA'S CHAPEL

Wp	Zn	North	East
1	SO	86119	28070
2	SO	86279	28481
3	SO	86438	28864
4	SO	87027	29606
5	SO	87132	29739
6	SO	87000	29875
7	SO	87058	29949
8	SO	86900	29868
9	SO	86763	29918
10	SO	86617	29746
11	SO	86165	29367
12	SO	85871	29175
13	SO	85588	28768
14	SO	85503	28385
15	SO	85463	28272
16	SO	84603	27841
17	SO	84466	27869
18	SO	85297	27514
19	SO	85421	27595
20	SO	85624	27732

9

UPTON UPON SEVERN

Wp	Zn	North	East
1	SO	85360	40661
2	SO	86170	40326
3	SO	86305	39343
4	SO	86101	38657
5	SO	85657	38721
6	SO	85164	38732
7	SO	84846	38626
8	SO	84602	39117
9	SO	84458	39205
10	SO	84618	39286
11	SO	84774	39616
12	SO	84703	40054
13	SO	84878	40166
14	SO	85093	40592

10

WORCESTER AND THE SEVERN

Wp	Zn	North	East
1	SO	88327	60194
2	SO	88192	60391
3	SO	88083	60493
4	SO	88027	60557
5	SO	87912	60716
6	SO	87743	60748
7	SO	87384	60721
8	SO	87171	61022
9	SO	86815	61075
10	SO	86528	60751
11	SO	86182	60624
12	SO	86175	60454
13	SO	85340	60690
14	SO	85142	60231
15	SO	84740	59961
16	SO	84355	60105
17	SO	84256	59959
18	SO	84317	59911
19	SO	84086	59702
20	SO	84015	59576
21	SO	83977	59643
22	SO	83738	59405
23	SO	83638	58823
24	SO	83695	58658
25	SO	83516	58215
26	SO	83487	57754
27	SO	83635	57631
28	SO	83877	57376
29	SO	84084	57096
30	SO	84174	56697
31	SO	84157	56514
32	SO	84028	56462
33	SO	84244	55282
34	SO	84619	54868
35	SO	84788	54938

11

WORCESTER AND ITS CANAL

Wp	Zn	North	East
1	SO	84785	54950
2	SO	84677	54818
3	SO	84892	54429
4	SO	85249	54399
5	SO	85514	55033
6	SO	85367	55466
7	SO	85042	56588
8	SO	88615	57575
9	SO	89642	58045
10	SO	89884	58822
11	SO	89813	59021
12	SO	89800	59221
13	SO	89759	59341
14	SO	89678	59732
15	SO	89654	59832
16	SO	89503	59795
17	SO	89373	59761
18	SO	89201	59807
19	SO	89008	59899
20	SO	88847	60069
21	SO	88291	60188

12

HANLEY CASTLE AND HANLEY SWAN

Wp	Zn	North	East
1	SO	83873	42010
2	SO	83732	42077
3	SO	83500	42258
4	SO	83382	42503
5	SO	83427	42775
6	SO	83504	42845

7	SO	83367	43239
8	SO	83161	43590
9	SO	82705	43845
10	SO	82450	43985
11	SO	81895	43941
12	SO	82083	44040
13	SO	81982	44363
14	SO	81676	44527
15	SO	81532	44487
16	SO	81319	44493
17	SO	81168	44681
18	SO	81120	44778
19	SO	80987	44990
20	SO	80905	44821
21	SO	80380	44425
22	SO	80469	44169
23	SO	80510	43992
24	SO	81285	42948
25	SO	81223	42588
26	SO	81618	42570
27	SO	81946	42545
28	SO	82055	42509
29	SO	82159	42522
30	SO	82284	42534
31	SO	82419	42524
32	SO	82516	42485
33	SO	82543	42109
34	SO	82906	41861
35	SO	83263	41745
36	SO	83399	41711
37	SO	83644	41497
38	SO	83738	41213
39	SO	83886	41268
40	SO	83904	41411
41	SO	83850	41504
42	SO	83873	41865

13

MADRESFIELD COURT

Wp	Zn	North	East
1	SO	82951	48723
2	SO	83128	48764
3	SO	84128	48567
4	SO	83898	48716
5	SO	83803	48409
6	SO	83850	47515
7	SO	83570	47101
8	SO	83424	46932
9	SO	83534	46827
10	SO	82981	46527
11	SO	82684	46778
12	SO	82471	46838
13	SO	82270	46958
14	SO	82114	46984
15	SO	81699	47183
16	SO	80948	47195
17	SO	80523	47015
18	SO	80401	47682
19	SO	80892	47847
20	SO	81319	48055
21	SO	82323	48238
22	SO	82478	48373
23	SO	82631	48533
24	SO	82725	48673

14

THE FULL MONTY

Wp	Zn	North	East
1	SO	75721	34895
2	SO	76107	35510
3	SO	75980	35896
4	SO	76151	35926
5	SO	75940	36431
6	SO	75879	36872
7	SO	75959	37520
8	SO	75840	37747
9	SO	75665	38017
10	SO	76025	38419
11	SO	76192	38574
12	SO	76198	39020
13	SO	76270	39465
14	SO	75994	39653
15	SO	75989	40031
16	SO	76333	40429
17	SO	76712	40863
18	SO	76837	41311
19	SO	76841	41861
20	SO	76790	42130
21	SO	76891	42506
22	SO	76910	43032
23	SO	76866	43718
24	SO	76904	44200
25	SO	76922	44738
26	SO	76886	45221
27	SO	76720	46176
28	SO	76940	46366
29	SO	76690	46806
30	SO	76803	46633
31	SO	76946	47045
32	SO	77041	46996

15

BETWEEN GREAT MALVERN AND COLWALL STATIONS

Wp	Zn	North	East
1	SO	78292	45688
2	SO	78404	45457
3	SO	78259	45211
4	SO	78174	45298
5	SO	78023	44502
6	SO	78069	44221
7	SO	77927	44093
8	SO	77630	43330
9	SO	77247	43440
10	SO	77202	43180
11	SO	77130	42883
12	SO	77107	42960
13	SO	76881	42702
14	SO	76759	42374
15	SO	76582	42064
16	SO	76478	42104
17	SO	76504	42198
18	SO	76273	42243
19	SO	76004	42285
20	SO	75951	42412
21	SO	75642	42456

16

NORTH HILL FROM LINK COMMON

Wp	Zn	North	East
1	SO	77888	47051
2	SO	77747	46935
3	SO	77654	46947
4	SO	77322	46931
5	SO	76985	47045
6	SO	76943	47026
7	SO	76898	46895
8	SO	76819	46630
9	SO	76938	46665
10	SO	76803	46487
11	SO	76778	46390
12	SO	76941	46369
13	SO	76733	46177
14	SO	77072	45922
15	SO	77216	45809
16	SO	77229	46058
17	SO	77328	46169
18	SO	77404	46407
19	SO	77543	46425
20	SO	77608	46651

17

WORCESTERSHIRE BEACON

Wp	Zn	North	East
1	SO	77160	43508
2	SO	76985	43741
3	SO	76879	43838
4	SO	76894	44027
5	SO	76916	44478
6	SO	76912	44743
7	SO	76883	45225
8	SO	76871	45455
9	SO	76827	45676
10	SO	76947	45799
11	SO	76892	45825
12	SO	77233	45795
13	SO	77337	45587
14	SO	77377	45122
15	SO	77340	44759
16	SO	77224	44137

18

HOLYWELL AND THE KETTLE SINGS

Wp	Zn	North	East
1	SO	77199	43184
2	SO	77127	42891
3	SO	77103	42953
4	SO	77056	43125

Wp	Zn	North	East
5	SO	76877	42706
6	SO	76798	42399
7	SO	76592	42063
8	SO	76478	42103
9	SO	76758	41892
10	SO	76768	41715
11	SO	76765	41523
12	SO	76797	41486
13	SO	76942	41352
14	SO	76872	41496
15	SO	77083	42008
16	SO	77018	42320
17	SO	77058	42730

19

HEREFORDSHIRE BEACON FROM CASTLEMORTON COMMON

Wp	Zn	North	East
1	SO	78683	38804
2	SO	78703	38953
3	SO	77353	38422
4	SO	76701	38781
5	SO	76757	39042
6	SO	76718	39209
7	SO	76341	39387
8	SO	76216	39487
9	SO	76242	39379
10	SO	75994	39659
11	SO	75976	40030
12	SO	76306	40409
13	SO	76514	39994
14	SO	76679	39770
15	SO	76944	39828
16	SO	77284	39545
17	SO	78044	39499
18	SO	78425	39341

20

CASTLEMORTON TUMP

Wp	Zn	North	East
1	SO	78691	38778
2	SO	78734	38498
3	SO	79452	38258
4	SO	79332	37910
5	SO	79226	37666
6	SO	79405	37335
7	SO	79468	37290
8	SO	79427	37170
9	SO	79511	37136
10	SO	79644	37091
11	SO	80045	36939
12	SO	80179	36952
13	SO	80265	36974
14	SO	80399	36816
15	SO	80746	36985
16	SO	80932	37129
17	SO	81132	37384
18	SO	80618	37797
19	SO	80632	38448
20	SO	80299	38553
21	SO	79069	38788
22	SO	79061	39012
23	SO	78801	39041

21

EASTNOR PARK TO LEDBURY

Wp	Zn	North	East
1	SO	75878	36876
2	SO	75809	37846
3	SO	75653	38017
4	SO	75235	37838
5	SO	75044	37868
6	SO	74336	37953
7	SO	73979	37938
8	SO	73771	37333
9	SO	73324	37225
10	SO	73151	37291
11	SO	72699	37220
12	SO	72533	37482
13	SO	71853	37705
14	SO	71597	37583
15	SO	71456	37675
16	SO	71097	37725

22

GULLET QUARRY AND MIDSUMMER HILL

Wp	Zn	North	East
1	SO	76640	38127
2	SO	76258	38016
3	SO	75661	38020
4	SO	75843	37744
5	SO	75959	37510
6	SO	75892	36873
7	SO	76375	36903
8	SO	76637	36805
9	SO	77317	37075
10	SO	77601	37086
11	SO	77257	37669
12	SO	77447	37847
13	SO	77745	38252
14	SO	77990	38044
15	SO	78591	37669
16	SO	78665	38031
17	SO	77772	38309
18	SO	77332	38401

23

RAGGED STONE AND CHASE END HILLS

Wp	Zn	North	East
1	SO	75894	36886
2	SO	75769	36799
3	SO	75914	36479
4	SO	76036	36080
5	SO	76152	35917
6	SO	76049	35918
7	SO	75735	34940
8	SO	76106	35511
9	SO	75986	35896
10	SO	76237	36818
11	SO	76117	36902

24

CRADLEY AND WEST MALVERN

Wp	Zn	North	East
1	SO	73533	47110
2	SO	73629	46885
3	SO	73809	46817
4	SO	73860	46621
5	SO	74060	46592
6	SO	74227	46445
7	SO	74282	46373
8	SO	74488	46316
9	SO	75095	46322
10	SO	75488	46294
11	SO	75731	46180
12	SO	76111	46190
13	SO	76289	46244
14	SO	76450	46228
15	SO	76645	46172
16	SO	77213	46451
17	SO	76682	46574
18	SO	76589	46708
19	SO	76530	47033
20	SO	76462	47041
21	SO	75976	46819
22	SO	75767	47094
23	SO	75460	47266
24	SO	75383	47340
25	SO	75013	47556
26	SO	74303	47595
27	SO	73804	47477

25

OLD STORRIDGE COMMON

Wp	Zn	North	East
1	SO	75099	52161
2	SO	75078	51747
3	SO	75248	51418
4	SO	75300	51300
5	SO	75317	51266
6	SO	75207	51055
7	SO	75269	50735
8	SO	75335	50620
9	SO	75457	50555
10	SO	75558	50465
11	SO	76099	49594
12	SO	76025	49570
13	SO	76013	49356
14	SO	75346	49808
15	SO	75118	49818
16	SO	75040	50041
17	SO	75032	50416
18	SO	75098	50597
19	SO	75005	51574
20	SO	74958	51466

21	SO	74504	51356
22	SO	74478	51370
23	SO	74900	51576
24	SO	74850	52015
25	SO	74834	52121

26

COLWALL CHURCH, OYSTER HILL AND LEDBURY

Wp	Zn	North	East
1	SO	73846	42271
2	SO	73172	42239
3	SO	72934	42131
4	SO	72605	41936
5	SO	72379	41825
6	SO	71961	40920
7	SO	71455	40779
8	SO	71128	40021
9	SO	71099	39671
10	SO	71008	39359
11	SO	71212	38903
12	SO	71215	38642
13	SO	71196	38457
14	SO	71249	37891
15	SO	71135	37729
16	SO	71479	38507
17	SO	71564	38719
18	SO	71708	38957
19	SO	71640	39064
20	SO	72179	39925
21	SO	72338	40555
22	SO	72372	40783
23	SO	73051	40692
24	SO	73200	41551
25	SO	73497	41915

27

DAFFODIL WAY

Wp	Zn	North	East
1	SO	67793	28435
2	SO	67672	28932
3	SO	67392	28819
4	SO	66998	28821
5	SO	66864	28933
6	SO	66591	29225
7	SO	66283	29623
8	SO	66505	30513
9	SO	66587	30865
10	SO	66804	31076
11	SO	67002	31308
12	SO	67305	31551
13	SO	67654	31483
14	SO	67755	31361
15	SO	67986	31306
16	SO	68386	31110
17	SO	68309	30753
18	SO	68294	30594
19	SO	68795	30698
20	SO	68901	31173
21	SO	69111	31498
22	SO	69639	31664
23	SO	69748	31566
24	SO	70020	31322
25	SO	70070	31161
26	SO	70080	30879
27	SO	70309	30281
28	SO	70347	30049
29	SO	69943	29371
30	SO	69888	29263
31	SO	69497	28725
32	SO	69152	28577
33	SO	68285	28606
34	SO	67745	28856

28

AROUND HAUGH WOOD

Wp	Zn	North	East
1	SO	57788	38537
2	SO	58063	38530
3	SO	58355	38694
4	SO	58878	38761
5	SO	59005	38772
6	SO	59220	38461
7	SO	59345	38388
8	SO	59469	38290
9	SO	59515	38188
10	SO	59688	38137
11	SO	59560	37832
12	SO	59481	37741
13	SO	59344	37432
14	SO	59825	36377
15	SO	59744	36350
16	SO	59522	35934
17	SO	58853	35549
18	SO	58838	35316
19	SO	58923	35201
20	SO	58968	34817
21	SO	58953	34678
22	SO	58187	34424
23	SO	57942	34440
24	SO	57779	34601
25	SO	57814	34745
26	SO	57620	35532
27	SO	57370	36046
28	SO	57239	36232
29	SO	56977	36765
30	SO	57085	37040
31	SO	57170	37336
32	SO	57363	37319
33	SO	57465	37368
34	SO	57600	37562
35	SO	57932	38273
36	SO	57927	38543

29

FOWNHOPE AND CAPLER CAMP

Wp	Zn	North	East
1	SO	58437	31282
2	SO	58887	31706
3	SO	59088	32352
4	SO	59070	32434
5	SO	59100	32761
6	SO	59189	32877
7	SO	59537	32926
8	SO	59620	32987
9	SO	59737	33238
10	SO	59828	33384
11	SO	59830	33478
12	SO	59973	33607
13	SO	60073	33743
14	SO	60136	33836
15	SO	60108	33904
16	SO	59936	34029
17	SO	59888	34232
18	SO	59610	34466
19	SO	59516	34584
20	SO	59437	34623
21	SO	59210	34628
22	SO	58993	34751
23	SO	58073	34344
24	SO	57893	34423
25	SO	58012	34252
26	SO	57749	34081
27	SO	57550	33938
28	SO	57500	33877
29	SO	57266	33731
30	SO	57009	33617
31	SO	56882	33316
32	SO	56687	33058
33	SO	57039	32645
34	SO	57584	32766
35	SO	58246	32715
36	SO	58749	32731
37	SO	58726	32812
38	SO	58566	31595

30

MAY HILL

Wp	Zn	North	East
1	SO	70967	21359
2	SO	70933	21423
3	SO	70359	20872
4	SO	70157	20689
5	SO	70021	20754
6	SO	69859	20844
7	SO	69396	21815
8	SO	69614	22134
9	SO	69791	22322
10	SO	69987	22710
11	SO	70013	23062
12	SO	70253	23187
13	SO	70874	23241
14	SO	70978	22704
15	SO	71022	22442
16	SO	70984	22406
17	SO	70939	22143
18	SO	70978	22053
20	SO	70805	21599

APPENDICES

APPENDIX A PUBLIC TRANSPORT

Each walk description includes a section detailing how that route can be accessed by public transport. Here I've brought them together in summary, to help with planning.

WALK NUMBER/TITLE	BUS Nº
1 Bredon Hill from Westmancote	540 from **Tewkesbury** or **Evesham**
2 Overbury	540 from **Tewkesbury** or **Evesham**
3 Elmley Castle	540 from **Tewkesbury** or **Evesham**
4 Woollas Hall	382 from **Worcester**
5 Eckington Bridge	382 from **Worcester**
6 Pershore Bridge and Tiddesley Wood	550 from **Worcester**
7 The Severn and The Avon	351 from **Upton upon Severn** or **Tewkesbury**
8 Odda's Chapel	351 from **Upton upon Severn** or **Tewkesbury**
9 Upton upon Severn	362 or 363 from **Great Malvern**
10 Worcester and The Severn	44, 44A, 44B or 45 from **Great Malvern**
11 Worcester and its Canal	44, 44A, 44B or 45 from **Great Malvern**
12 Hanley Castle & Hanley Swan	363 from **Great Malvern**
13 Madresfield Court	363 from **Great Malvern**
14 The Full Monty	Starts from **Great Malvern**
15 Between Great Malvern and Colwall Stations	Starts from **Great Malvern**
16 North Hill from Link Common	Starts from **Great Malvern**
17 Worcestershire Beacon	362 or 363 from **Great Malvern**
18 Holywell & 'The Kettle Sings'	362 or 363 from **Great Malvern**
19 Herefordshire Beacon from Castlemorton Common	362 or 363 from **Great Malvern**
20 Castlemorton Tump	362 or 363 from **Great Malvern**
21 Eastnor Park	675 from **Great Malvern**
22 Gullet Quarry & Midsummer Hill	362 or 363 from **Great Malvern**
23 Ragged Stone and Chase End Hills	no bus option
24 Cradley and West Malvern	Walk starts from **Great Malvern**

25 Old Storridge Common — **417** from **Ledbury** or **Worcester**

26 Colwall Church, Oyster Hill & Ledbury — **675** from **Great Malvern**

27 The Daffodil Way — **132** from **Ledbury** or **Gloucester**

28 Around Haugh Wood — **453** from **Hereford**

29 Fownhope and Capler Camp — **453** from **Hereford**

30 May Hill — **33** from **Gloucester**

APPENDIX B WHERE TO STAY

For a wide choice of accommodation visit **www.great-malvern.co.uk**

I have personal experience of the following and am happy to recommend them.

Cottage in the Wood, Holywell Road, **Malvern Wells** WR14 4LG
- a sumptuous hotel with superb food and magnificent views.
01684 588860 www.cottageinthewood.co.uk

The Old Coach House, 208, Wells Road, **Malvern Wells** WR14 4HD
- traditional bed & breakfast.
01684 564832 www.coachhousemalvern.co.uk

The Turbles, Druggers End Lane, **Castlemorton** WR13 6JD
- self-catering chalets in a beautiful, quiet setting.
07963 414613 www.turbles.co.uk

The Marlbank Inn, Marlbank Road, **Welland** WR13 6NA
- campsite attached to pub, child friendly and good pub grub.
01684 310603 www.marlbankinn.co.uk

Close to **Bredon Hill**:-

The Anchor Inn, Eckington WR10 3BA
- good value bed and breakfast attached to a pub.
01386 750356 www.anchoreckington.co.uk

The Moretons, Bredon GL20 7EN
- superb rural self-catering accommodation complete with swimming pool.
01684 772294 www.moretons-soutar.co.uk